Who Cares?

Who Cares?

Public Ambivalence
and Government Activism
from the New Deal
to the Second Gilded Age

Katherine S. Newman
and Elisabeth S. Jacobs

Princeton University Press   •   Princeton and Oxford

Copyright © 2010 by Princeton University Press

Published by Princeton University Press, 41 William Street, Princeton, New Jersey 08540

In the United Kingdom: Princeton University Press, 6 Oxford Street,

Woodstock, Oxfordshire OX20 1TW

All Rights Reserved

Library of Congress Cataloging-in-Publication Data

Newman, Katherine S., 1953–

Who cares? : public ambivalence and government activism

from the New Deal to the second gilded age /

Katherine S. Newman, Elisabeth S. Jacobs.

p. cm.

Includes bibliographical references and index.

ISBN 978-0-691-13563-2 (hardcover : alk. paper)

1. United States—Economic policy—20th century.

2. United States—Politics and government—1933–1945.

3. United States—Politics and government—1945–1989.

I. Jacobs, Elisabeth S., 1977–   II. Title.

HC106.N64 2010   338.973—dc22   2009029407

British Library Cataloging-in-Publication Data is available

This book has been composed in Electra LT Std

Printed on acid-free paper. ∞

press.princeton.edu

Printed in the United States of America

1 3 5 7 9 10 8 6 4 2

For the Honorable Edward M. Kennedy

Lion of the Senate,
who devoted his career to making government work
for the nation's most vulnerable people.

Contents

Illustrations

Note: We rely on a variety of source for public opinion data throughout this volume, with Gallup and National Election Studies surveys doing much of the heavy lifting. Gallup data is available online through the Roper Center's Public Opinion Archives, a subscription-based library of public opinion data (see http://www.ropercenter.uconn.edu/). Data from the National Election Studies are available for free downloading online (see http://www.electionstudies.org/).

Tables

Acknowledgments

This book initially came into the world as a contribution to a conference organized by Professors David Rothman of Columbia University and Howard Rosenthal of New York University, with the support of the Open Society Institute. They asked the participants to think about the question of what we owe one another, a topic neither of us had devoted much attention to until their invitation landed in the email inbox. We are grateful to them and to the participants in that conference, most especially Adam Berinsky of the Massachusetts Institute of Technology, whose feedback was instrumental in shaping this book. Indeed, without the careful work Adam has done to redress the limitations of the opinion polls of the 1930s and 1940s, we would not have embarked on this project at all.

The encouragement we received from colleagues in Princeton's Politics Department—Larry Bartels, Marty Gilens, and Nolan McCarty—was more instrumental than they know in pushing us to turn our conference presentation into a book. Since all three of them make use of public opinion data as their bread and butter, while neither of us typically does, their interest in the original paper inspired us to dig a little deeper. Julian Zelizer of Princeton's History Department and Bob Kuttner, editor of *The American Prospect*, were good enough to set their own important work aside long enough to critique the first draft of this book, and we appreciate the insights they contributed. Cybelle Fox, of the University of California, Berkeley, gave that draft the most thorough review imaginable and pushed us to refine our analysis of public support for Roosevelt's policies. We appreciate her exacting standards and thank her for the detailed input she provided. We are also grateful to three anonymous reviewers who provided helpful advice, particularly in conceptualizing resistance to the policy directions set by the administrations we discuss in this book.

Max Fraser, a recent graduate of the Department of History at the University of Pennsylvania and a current staff member of *The Nation*, was dogged in his pursuit of the archival materials we needed to understand what ordinary people tried to communicate to the White House during the New Deal and the Great Society era, and in the course of the ill-fated debates over the Family Assistance Plan during the Nixon administration. With the help of the dedicated staff at the Roosevelt Presidential Archives in Hyde Park, New York, the Johnson Library in Austin, Texas, and the Nixon Archives in Washington, D.C., we were able to sample from the proponents and the detractors, the policy "in crowd" and the distant outsiders in the hinterlands, to learn something more of the texture of public attitudes than can be gleaned from polls.

Special thanks go to Steven Attewell, a doctoral candidate in the history of public policy at the University of California, Santa Barbara, and an authority on the history of public employment and on the New Deal more generally, for correcting more errors than we care to remember. His enthusiastic support and attention to detail pointed us in the right direction on many occasions.

At Princeton University, Katherine Newman is the beneficiary of generous support from the Woodrow Wilson School's Faculty Research Fund, which financed the research for this book and the time devoted to it by her assistant, Nancy Turco. Elisabeth Jacobs completed much of the work for this book during her years as a fellow of the National Science Foundation's Multidisciplinary Program on Inequality and Social Policy at Harvard University. She is also appreciative of the time she was able to sequester to complete this manuscript during her year as the American Sociological Association Congressional Fellow and the gracious understanding of her colleagues on the Senate Committee on Health, Education, Labor and Pensions.

Both of us are grateful for the encouragement we received from beginning to end from Eric Schwartz at Princeton University Press and the rest of his colleagues, whose hard work makes the Press one of the jewels in the university's crown.

This book is dedicated to the late Senator Edward Kennedy, chair of the Senate Committee on Health, Education, Labor and Pensions, whose lifelong commitment to the well-being of the nation's least fortunate citizens is testimonial to how much a progressive vision matters. His efforts to increase funding for health care, college education, unemployment insurance, and many other critical benefits for the poor remind us all of what a real leader can do with the right moral compass.

Who Cares?

Introduction
Devoted to the Common Good?

President Barack Obama inherited an economic crisis as severe as any we have known since the Great Depression, and many have likened his task to Franklin D. Roosevelt's. Indeed, the appeal to the 1930s and FDR's heroic rescue of the nation has been invoked many times as a model for the challenge Obama faces. From the West Wing "brain trust" of the Obama administration to the investment in public employment, there are many parallels to the Depression experience. Yet the present crisis takes place against a backdrop of rampant inequality and a legacy of political polarization that make any social compact of the kind expressed in the New Deal harder to jump-start.

Social critics often remark on the declining commitment to the common good in our era. The wealthy, who have benefited disproportionately from the economic growth of the last forty years, have pulled so far away from the middle—not to mention the bottom—that they no longer consider themselves bound by the social contract. During the long period of conservative dominance, the commitments of citizens toward one another eroded in the face of the more resonant message of individual accountability and self-advantage. Confidence in the efficacy of government all but disappeared.

From this vantage point, commentators tell us, the past appears more appealing. The New Deal and the Great Society stand out as periods when we made good on the idea that citizens should be sworn to the common good and the protection of the needy. As Michael Tomasky put the matter in *The American Prospect,*

For many years—during their years of dominance and success, the period of the New Deal up through the first part of the Great Society—the Democrats practiced a brand of liberalism quite different from today's. Yes, it certainly sought to expand both rights and prosperity. But it did something more: The liberalism was built around the idea—the philosophical principle—that citizens should be called upon to look beyond their own self-interest and work for a great common interest.[1]

The New Deal, Tomasky tells us, "engaged and ennobled people." It gave us Social Security, rural electrification, federal mortgage insurance, and public works ranging from a federal highway system to thousands of new schools. That same expansive and inclusive spirit later animated American generosity on an international scale through the Marshall Plan. John F. Kennedy asked "for sacrifice for the common good." Lyndon Johnson's Great Society sprang from the same civic republican roots. Tomasky urges us to reconnect with this great tradition to reinvigorate the country, an admonition addressed especially to the Democratic Party.

But is it correct to think of the New Deal era as a time when the public determined that we owe one another a lot? Or was it a case of policy triumphing over public sentiment and of social policies that were more generous than popular? Our analysis, presented at length in chapter one, is that Roosevelt encountered a great deal of resistance toward many aspects of the New Deal. Much of the backlash developed as the fiscal bite of the New Deal became clearer and, ironically, as some of its boldest programs reduced unemployment, leading some to question the need to continue government spending on such a large scale. But even at the outset, before we had the opinion polls of the kind that reveal the public's reservations, letters to the president and the first lady make it clear that the American people were divided about the promise of the New Deal. Far from being sympathetic to the poor, much popular opinion held that the unemployed were the authors of their own misfortune, that recipients of government benefits were cheaters and loafers who would have little trouble finding work if they really wanted it. Attempts to rescue them through federal programs were creating helpless, dependent masses that would never stand on their own two feet. While many, perhaps even the majority, were desperate for FDR's intervention, others, often in elite and powerful circles, were adamantly opposed on ideological and moral grounds. FDR prevailed over these critics, but the struggle forced him to compromise in ways that excited even more criticism and denied benefits to millions of Americans, who had to wait decades before their legitimate claims were recognized.

And what of Johnson's Great Society: did the initial support for government investment in employment and training, nutrition, housing, and health care for the poor last? Or did Johnson sustain mandates despite growing public opposition? In chapter two we argue that as long as programs for the needy were understood to benefit the deserving poor—widows and their children—their public image was mildly positive.[2] But the moment those worthies were removed and public programs were directed toward the able-bodied—never-married mothers, abandoned wives, and above all minorities—public support evaporated, and hostility toward the undeserving festered.[3] To some degree it was always there. Yet in a period of growing affluence, neither the cost of the programs nor the ways in which they stretched public patience for a "brother's keeper" role for government were particularly visible. Johnson faced more indifference than opposition, at least in the beginning. But a groundswell of public frustration eventually reached his White House as well, inspired by a belief in the centrality of the work ethic and the corollary that those who stand outside the labor market deserve their poverty.

That negative impulse was strengthened by the urban riots of the 1960s and the rise of the black power movement, which raised the visibility of African American grievances against a society riddled with discrimination and inequality, and coincided with—perhaps fueled—a backlash against much of what the Great Society stood for. Nonetheless, Johnson persevered, and as a result, today we have Medicaid and Medicare, Head Start, food stamps, and a variety of other manifestations of his social activism. That legislative record inspires today's progressives to regard the 1960s as a period of civic renewal, and rightly so. But the War on Poverty was not spurred by public opinion; it was forged by a leader willing to move out ahead of his constituents. When the opposition grew, LBJ was willing to swim against the stream. One could say the same—and we do—about Richard Nixon, hardly a hero of the Left. Yet Nixon's domestic policy contained surprisingly progressive elements that were almost entirely rejected by the public at large and left a legacy from which those at the bottom have actually benefited more than we often credit.

Is this divide between leaders and their constituents evident only in periods we remember as progressive? Fast-forward to the 1980s and '90s and the triumph of the conservative revolution, and we meet the disjunction once again. Presidents Reagan, George H. W. Bush, and George W. Bush were bent on reversing the legacy of the New Deal, rolling back government efforts at social engineering wherever possible.

Given the sustained period of conservative activism, we might imagine enthusiastic and growing public support for a limited conception of government intervention on behalf of the weakest members of society. Our analysis in chapter three suggests otherwise, for the conservative electoral victories took place against a backdrop of rising inequality, runaway CEO salaries, and, beginning in the early 1980s, a tidal wave of outsourcing and downsizing that shook the middle class badly.[4] Blue-collar workers felt the brunt of deindustrialization first, but by the early 1980s it was the white-collar managers who began to see their prospects wash away.

Popular sentiment was ambivalent about some of the most fervent convictions of conservative politicians. Their victories at the ballot box diverted attention from the quiet *increase* in public support for policies that dampened inequality and protected the less fortunate. The economic meltdown that gathered force in late 2008 exacerbated growing vulnerabilities among educated, experienced workers. We argue that instability among working families, including those that are relatively well off, is now so great and the prospects for the next generation are so uncertain that a kind of tolerance for, if not an embrace of, government support for the poor has replaced the harder-hearted temperament of the 1930s and 1960s. Indeed, Barack Obama's election is explained, at least in part, by the desire for greater protection from the unchecked power of the market as championed by many conservatives.

In this book, we argue that in these three periods of our history, political leaders often moved boldly into a policy vacuum or forged on against growing antagonism. They pushed and pulled legislators into creating and then sustaining the progressive history of the 1930s and 1960s we now—mistakenly—see as a sea change in popular political culture. Indeed, one of the reasons why presidential speeches given by Roosevelt and Johnson stand as among the most powerful and moving in American history is because they were trying to *catalyze* or *recapture* popular sentiment in the "brother's keeper" direction when it was in danger of listing the opposite way. Similarly, from the 1980s to the election of Barack Obama, the rhetorical rejection of "Washington," the identification of government as the source of our economic problems rather than as part of the solution, was sustained even as the public moved—modestly, to be sure—in the other direction.

To illustrate the disconnect between the brother's keeper sentiments we remember and the reality of limits to public endorsement of government activism on behalf of the less fortunate, we turn to opinion polls and letters to leaders for each of the three key periods: the New Deal Era of the 1930s and the early 1940s, the Great Society and Johnson's War on Poverty, and the "second gilded age" of the 1980s and 1990s, when income inequality grew rapidly and an ascendant conservative movement unraveled many of the programs and policies born and nurtured in the previous two eras.

In the 1930s, a series of surveys was undertaken by magazines like *Forbes* and *Fortune* to gauge public views of the Depression and to assess the public's reactions to the New Deal. The first public opinion firms, led by Roper and Gallup, joined in this effort to measure public sympathy (or antipathy) toward FDR's plans. These polls were well known to the Roosevelt administration and, as we note in chapter one, were critical to the president's understanding of just how far, how radically, he could push the federal government to respond to the economic crisis. But they have been little analyzed by scholars, despite the wealth of information they contain on the public's view of relief programs, Social Security, medical care, and the like, because they were not gathered according to modern standards of sampling.[5]

Thanks to methodological interventions developed by MIT political scientist Adam Berinsky, we are able to correct for their defects now and hence can mine many of these polls to understand more accurately what ordinary Americans thought about the causes of poverty and unemployment, what they believed the government should or should not do about the maelstrom of the Depression, and whether or not the particular circumstances of their own lives or the condition of their communities mattered in shaping their views.[6] Were communities that were particularly hard hit by shuttered factories and grim breadlines more sympathetic to the developing welfare state? Or did they turn a hard face to the needy, believing that federal benefits would coddle the poor and turn them into lifelong dependents, unable to fend for themselves? What about those who were on relief themselves? How different were their views from those of their more fortunate neighbors or the readers of *Fortune* magazine? The 400-plus opinion polls of the New Deal era give us some purchase on the answers.

But numbers tell only part of the story. For more textured insight, we turn to the voluminous correspondence that men and women all over the country sent to FDR, Eleanor Roosevelt, and the agencies that ministered to the poor and the unemployed. In the dark days of the thirties, people who had virtually nothing to their names—the millions of Joads drifting away from failing farms, the desperate blue-collar men shuffling around outside the shuttered factories—were eager to let their leaders know what they thought. The Roosevelt archives in Hyde Park contain thousands of letters imploring the president and the First Lady to preserve or jettison the core programs of the New Deal.[7] We do not pretend to offer a random sample of these letters. We do make every effort to represent the variety of views locked away in the presidential archives and the letters written to Boake Carter, a Philadelphia radio announcer whose original claim to fame was his coverage of the Lindberg baby kidnapping but who devoted much of his broadcasting career to denouncing the New Deal.[8]

We take a similar approach to the 1960s, the second expansive period of government efforts to eradicate poverty. The opinion polls we analyze, coupled with letters contained in the Johnson and Nixon archives, continue a conversation about who is deserving that began thirty years earlier, in the depths of the Depression, and continued at high decibels as the Great Society developed and the debate over Nixon's ideas for the negative income tax became part of the policy lexicon.

Finally, we turn to the General Social Survey and the National Election Studies for the 1980s and 1990s to understand how the people have diverged from their elected leaders in the context of galloping inequality, increasingly unstable employment for the middle class (as well as those below), and dimming prospects for intergenerational mobility.

To be sure, public opinion is not the only source of pressure on presidential leadership. Elites with special access, organized interest groups, social movements that gathered the allegiance of the downtrodden, marches on Washington—all of these other ways of expressing the public mindset surely played an important role in shaping policymakers' ultimate decisions. In this book, we focus attention on what opinion polls and letters to political leaders can tell us about the limits and contours of American attitudes toward government intervention on behalf of the poor. All of the presidents we consider here tracked the findings of opinion surveys, even in FDR's era, when the practice of polling was in its infancy. It is beyond our mission—though a worthy question—to determine how leaders weighed the force of public opinion as measured in polls against the more dramatic and visible evidence of popular movements and marches.

What we hope to do instead is focus on what the surveys tell us about mass attitudes.[9] In all three periods, the public exhibited far more mixed and contentious attitudes about activist government than the politicians they returned to office. This does not mean the leaders were totally indifferent to the popular will. On the contrary, the advisers in Roosevelt's Brain Trust tempered their ambitious rescue plans because they understood that the public rejected many of their ideas. Roosevelt himself was no fan of the dole. He had doubts about boosting federal spending in the form supported by adherents of Keynesian economics, and his decision to slam on the brakes in 1937 in order to balance the budget provoked a brutal increase in unemployment. Administrator Harry Hopkins, head of various emergency relief programs and ultimately secretary of commerce, always believed in public employment as the answer to desperation, but he had to defend it in the face of mounting deficits that might have been partially ameliorated by a less expensive but wildly unpopular cash relief. Americans were more enthusiastic about federal employment programs than about the dole, but, as we show in chapter one, opposition to most forms of government help for the indigent was surprisingly strong, even in the states hardest hit by the calamity of the Depression.

Lyndon Johnson was as committed as Bobby Kennedy to the eradication of poverty. But while Kennedy appealed to the shame of Appalachian shacks in the richest nation on earth, Johnson spoke about the role of government in addressing educational preparation for the poor, to enable them to find a place in the working world. Work was the mantra, and in invoking it, LBJ was speaking to the popular belief in the sanctity of employment as an indirect means of addressing the poverty problem. Even so, as our analysis in chapter two shows, while Johnson benefited from a level of public indifference at the beginning of his term (into which he could insert the Great Society), he encountered growing opposition as time wore on. The achievements for which we remember the Great Society, particularly Medicare and Medicaid, not only failed to catalyze a groundswell of support, they faced declining public support over time.

Unlike Harry Hopkins, who followed up a similar commitment to the eradication of the deep poverty of the Depression with public jobs, Johnson did almost nothing to create employment, instead wrapping the Great Society around the objective of increasing educational opportunity and removing racial barriers to fair competition. These were worthy objectives, to be sure, but they were defined by a goal of fair play in education and labor markets, not by the creation of a universal social welfare system.[10] And even these less radical objectives were a hard sell in a country that was often ambivalent about the goals of the Great Society.

Where Richard Nixon advocated the negative income tax, which *was* a redistributive plan, Ronald Reagan's fondest wish was to strip government to its barest bones and foster Darwinian self-reliance as the answer to poverty. George W. Bush took this spirit further, enacting massive tax cuts for the rich and running up staggering deficits in line with what Reagan's budget director David Stockman argued would "starve the beast" and force an end to social programs of all kinds, including those for the poor. Though the public returned Bush to office, the opinion polls we examine in chapter three make it clear they did not swallow his vision whole. Conservative electoral triumphs of recent decades did not *respond* to public outcry to reverse direction; instead, they tried to *create* an ardor for dismantling government. To the extent that the proof lies in the ballot box, they succeeded—at least temporarily. But when we look for deep tracks in public opinion, the evidence is either meager or nonexistent that welfare state retrenchment and unfettered individualism were consonant with American attitudes.

In short, in the 1930s and 1960s, government officials created programs that encountered resistance in the court of public opinion and persevered in laying a foundation for the American welfare state that, although weak when compared with the social democracies of Europe, became an essential source of protection against the vagaries of the market. Leaders were politically courageous in the face of public sentiment that could have completely derailed the development or the persistence of the safety net.

In the 1980s and 1990s, conservatives were again bucking a tide, but one that was much harder to discern because the transformations wrought by globalization, declining union density, and skill-biased technological change produced a jarring set of realities whose causes and consequences are hotly debated even today. What the public registered in the polls, as we present in the third chapter, was a growing discontent with the runaway rich and a desire to sustain rather than dismantle the protections built during the New Deal and reinforced by the Great Society. This may be the best explanation for the election outcome of 2008, in which the conservative revolution seems to have come a cropper. If so, it will follow in the footsteps of other periods of extreme inequality, such as the Gilded Age of the late nineteenth century, in which political economies run amok ultimately provoked the election of progressive leaders promising change.

The essence of leadership is not registering the popular will and transforming it into policy but setting a course and sticking to one's guns in the face of growing resistance. This, we argue, is the real story of the New Deal, the Great Society, and the conservative triumph in the age of inequality.

1 Dissent and the New Deal

In the ranks of quite a few of the middle class white collar people and upwards, the mental havoc is pretty bad. Nobody really seems to feel that he is actually going to get an honest-to-goodness job or work in a hurry.

—Julian Claff, *writing from Philadelphia*

There is an increasing feeling of despair—the feeling that they will never get their jobs back. . . . The winter shut-down of so many of these [work relief] projects brings men into headquarters begging that the county road work be continued through this winter.

—Martha B. Bruere and Ernestine Ball,
writing from Schenectady, N.Y.

I think there is a terrible problem here of salvaging human material; or letting it permanently rot. . . . Present relief is a kind of hypodermic; it doesn't take long to realize that this ailment is chronic and needs long-time constructive planning to retrain these people and re-establish them.

—Martha Gellhorn, *writing from South Carolina*

The president of the Braddock National Bank said that if relief were withdrawn before work comes to the steel towns there would be rioting. I believe there would be in Duquense.

—Hazel Reavis, *writing from Braddock-Duquense, Pa.*

The morale of the jobless, generally, is bad. . . . It is my conviction that any drastic curtailment of relief in Chicago in the face of continued unemployment would provoke demonstrations of a violent nature.

—Thomas Steep, *writing from Chicago*[1]

In March 1935, Franklin D. Roosevelt hired a group of journalists to provide him with firsthand impressions of the toll the Great Depression was taking on the country and the impact of his New Deal programs on the lives of ordinary people. Stationed in small towns and big cities in every region of the country, the reporters wrote back with these discouraging accounts. Hopelessness, despair, and anger threatened to metastasize into widespread disorder.

As historian Irving Bernstein notes in his study of American workers, in the 1920s and 1930s, "unrest, frequently under Communist leadership, erupt[ed] into violence and rootless veterans [of the First World War] in quest of government handouts."[2] This social disorder led many to believe that the United States was on the brink of a revolt not unlike the Russian Revolution (then less than twenty years in the past). Looking back from the vantage point of the late 1950s, Arthur Schlesinger Jr. deemed the period leading up to the New Deal the "valley of darkness" and argued that the nation was prone to a violent upheaval.[3] In letters ordinary citizens sent to FDR, we see why Schlesinger came to this dire prediction. "It is now nearly two years since you pledged yourself to an attempt at bettering the lot of the 'forgotten man,'" Mrs. Carl Brenden of Laurel, Montana, reminded the president in her letter of 1934:

> As far as I can see the "forgotten man" is as forgotten as he ever was during the previous administrations. It is becoming increasingly apparent that slow starvation and attendant degradation is to be the lot of millions of forgotten men under either of the major parties and that we must look to the more radical groups for any relief.[4]

Why were ordinary people suffering? Views on this question divided the nation. For those on the right, Depression "losers" were experiencing the natural consequences of their own moral collapse and a decline in the work ethic, and were developing an unholy expectation for handouts at taxpayers' expense. For those at the other end of the ideological spectrum, the Depression was caused by the excessive, concentrated power of elites who were looking out for their own interests, ready to crush the common man if he got in the way. The Left urged Roosevelt to take radical action to curb the control of employers and redistribute wealth; the Right looked to Roosevelt to let the market exert its discipline. While millions of desperate families in the middle deemed the president a secular savior, and reelected him four times to underline the point, in its day the Roosevelt administration was pounded by critics on all sides. The dissension comes through in the opinion polls and letters to FDR on which we rely here.

Historian Lizbeth Cohen's study of Chicago's working class in the 1930s provides a vivid portrait of the turmoil that spread throughout the country as the crisis deepened.[5] In *Making a New Deal*, she notes that the rising tide of unemployment soon overwhelmed the traditional ethnic charities and the institutions of welfare capitalism as firms buckled under the pressure of bankruptcy.[6] Local organizations that had been able to cope with previous downturns watched helplessly as their constituents were evicted, the ranks of the "Hoover Hobos" swelled, and fathers were thrown out of work, only to find themselves dependent on the meager wages of their wives and children.[7]

The breakdown of the usual mechanisms for coping with economic downturns gave way to increasing expectations for federal assistance and spurred the creation of Roosevelt's New Deal, an unprecedented intervention by the federal government in labor markets, factory production, credit, construction, and housing. Money flowed into an alphabet soup of relief agencies that assumed unprecedented regulatory authority and organized agencies that did everything from build roads and schools to sew clothing and distribute food. In no other period of American history did the role of the state grow as fast as it did in the dark days of the 1930s.[8]

The Federal Emergency Relief Act, enacted in 1933, forked over $3.1 billion to states and localities to develop public works during the two years it was in operation. The Civil Works Administration (CWA) was one of its first programs and, although short-lived, the $400 million it spent put more than four million unemployed workers back on the job in the space of nine months. Men employed through the largesse of this and related programs, including the

Civilian Conservation Corps (CCC), understood full well whom they had to thank for the opportunity:

> Personally, you have made it possible, for me, through the CWA to get steady work for nine weeks, through the toughest time in the year, when I am practically at wits' end. I, my family, my immediate neighbors, stand fully behind your program, the NRA [National Recovery Administration], and anything that you may sponsor.[9] (Max Baron, Cleveland, Ohio, Dec. 11, 1933)

> Yesterday I celebrated my thirty-second birthday. It was the happiest birthday I have had for many years. I had been out of work for a long time. But now I have work through the CWA. I have two little children to take care of. . . . I am not an educated man but you do not think only of that class. You have been a blessing to the American people every where.[10] (John Binkley, Nashville, Tenn., Jan. 31, 1934)

> All of the projects you have sponsored have been a blessing to our people. The CCC and the NIRA [National Industrial Recovery Act] . . . have proven master strokes in keeping the people steady. The SERA [State Emergency Relief Administration] project has been the most wonderful of all. I know some people have not kept faith with you in aiding the people of this nation but that in no way detracts from the purpose of real relief.[11] (Rovaida T. Murray, San Diego, Calif., Mar. 17, 1935)

Others were not quite as appreciative. From the left, FDR was hit with the critique that he was too easy on business, too compliant in the face of demands to keep the wages of public workers low. Derogatory terms like "wage slavery" were thrown at relief work, which was in full swing by the time these letters from 1934 were placed in the White House mailbox. "You come along with this works relief bill and . . . demand that every man live on $50 a month," one writer from Henrickson, Indiana, complained. Another wrote,

There is a widespread public opinion, especially among the 12,000 unemployed and their dependents that this Administration may go the way that Hoover's battalions went . . . [if it doesn't do more to help the] 30,000,000 people, after five years, are still struggling with unemployment, starvation, and industrial bondage.[12] (B. A. Bonte, Bellevue, Ky., May 8, 1934)

What has, and what is, the administration and a democratic Congress doing to give reemployment to nearly a million men and their NOW POVERTY STRICKEN families who have been forced to wander in the valley of darkness and despair for going on four years?[13] (O. Caswell, Kansas City, Mo., Apr. 18, 1934; emphasis in original)

Though we remember Roosevelt today as the man who did more for the poor and dispossessed than any president before, and arguably anyone since, in his own day leftists and labor liberals often complained that Roosevelt's actions were too little, too late, and too tepid:

Your promise to limit immense fortunes and to redistribute the wealth—the only common sense solution for unemployment and over-production—has not been kept. In fact, it seems that the wealth has been further concentrated under your administration.[14] (V. Lowell Bronn, Rochester, Minn., Mar. 8, 1935)

Pardon me for suggesting again that government owned and controlled banks is the solution for the trouble we have and we must wipe out those vultures in Wall Street, Pittsburg, and other centers.[15] (S. H. Marsh, San Antonio, Tex., Sept. 29, 1934)

These complaints became more forceful as the expense of New Deal employment programs began to bite hard and the federal government considered cutting the wages below the $50 mark in the CWA, a forerunner of the better-known Works Progress Administration

(WPA). The proposed decrease "can mean but one thing," commented Harry Berg, a member of the Unemployed Industrial Workers of America:

> The betrayal of your office, your people, your country, of the oath you had made to them during election campaign, mainly, "to remember the forgotten man." . . . We demand that you take instant steps to see to it that the Civil Works Program is maintained, no further wage cuts or lay offs take place, and that all men laid off their jobs be reinstated—that you keep your pledge made to the "Forgotten Man", who has elected you.[16] (Cincinnati, Ohio, Feb. 17, 1934)

If the Left thought that FDR had done too little, the Right thought he had done far too much. Objections ran the gamut from ideological allergies to any form of government intrusion into the market to the conviction that even well-intentioned interventions ran the risk of undermining the work ethic. Laissez-faire advocates argued that the market functioned well only when left to its own devices. "Grievous as are the evils of poverty and unemployment," a Washington, D.C., newspaper editorial intoned, "the loss of individual freedom is an incomparably greater loss to mankind." The editorial continued,

> The sufferers are now turning in despair to the government and asking it to take charge of this vast machine, manage it for their benefit, and distribute the rewards among all. This presupposes a faith that history has never yet justified in the competence as well as in the good intentions of the men and women chosen by government, that is, by political methods, to govern and control the national economy.[17] (Sentinels of the Republic, Washington, D.C., May 8, 1933)

As fiscal conservatives saw it, government simply had no business involving itself in the world of commerce. This was partly a question of competence: politicians and policymakers, critics argued, simply did not know how to run the economy and were bound to make a mess of it. But for conservatives, and indeed for a fairly broad swath of public opinion, FDR's remedies for the Depression would cripple the discipline of the market:

> No country is stronger than its individual members and what we need is more rugged individualism and more real education and building up of character. Your continued interference in the function of natural business and social relations is ridiculous. These take care of themselves if left to flow freely along natural lines.[18] (Kenneth de Vos, Detroit, Mich., May 11, 1934)

From this perspective, government had no role to play in stabilizing an economy in free fall. Whatever momentary good might come out of FDR's interventions, they argued, would be more than overwhelmed by the long-term harm consequent on meddling, coddling, and disturbing the natural mechanisms of market self-correction. Two years into the New Deal, Roosevelt's conservative critics were railing against the destruction of the work ethic, even as federal programs cut unemployment nearly in half. "Don't you think it's time for a frank admission that your present path leads to destruction of what industry, brains, and hard work of the people of the United States have built over the last 150 years?" asked Charles Stephens of Rochester, New York:

> This country was built on individuality, and, true, while there have been some abuses, the result after all, speaks for itself. . . . The morale of our people is being destroyed through gifts by city, state and nation.[19] (Apr. 4, 1935)

Some of the angriest voices emerged from Americans who were trying to manage on their own through the maelstrom of the Depression and believed that FDR's remedies for other, less self-reliant, families were coming at their expense. "The forgotten man," Roy Eldridge (a letter writer from South Ardmore, Pennsylvania) lectured Roosevelt, "is NOT the shiftless, indifferent individual, who believes the world owe him a living (and is now getting it). The forgotten man in your administration is the thrifty middle class who have striven to make this country worth living in—whom you are striving to wipe out of existence."[20]

Eldridge's defiance was shared by many Americans who, though still employed, were struggling with the pressures of falling wages, foreclosures, and debt. The dole, they complained, was an unfair gift to the unemployed and undeserving. A letter from Burl Cross, a Lansing, Michigan, resident who described himself as a man "who wouldn't ask for relief if he needed it, who has raised his family by hard work and by the practice of the good old fashioned principles of pay-as-you-go and who has earned every dollar he ever spent, by his own efforts," makes the case to FDR in exactly these terms. "It is my considered opinion," Cross argued, "that you have done more to tear down the morale of the American people." He went on,

> You are penalizing over 90% of the people who have had to make their own way and earn a living and educate their families, so that you can sell all the loafers, ne'er-do-wells and never-would-worker type of people that the world owes them a living, with little or no effort on their part.[21] (July 2, 1936)

These refrains are all too familiar to modern ears, since they strongly resemble the complaints hurled at the welfare system and the provisions of the 2008 bailout plan to rescue delinquent home mortgage holders. Rather than view the down-and-out as worthy people temporarily in need of help, those who were fortunate enough to hold on to their homes and jobs deemed relief recipients slothful by definition. "There are hundreds of thousands of people like myself who have labored and denied themselves all their lives, who are now old, and very often ill," E. E. Denne of Los Angeles wrote to the president:

> Most of us would not accept public gratuities—they are the gift of providence to the profligate and lazy and foolish for the greater part, tho' to be sure, all these have votes, and no doubt in excess of the hard workers and self respectors.[22] (Nov. 23, no year)

Denne was in good company. A resident of Los Angeles wrote to Roosevelt to explain that he was at his wits' end with the all the taxes he had to pay, so much so that he wasn't sure it was worth it for him to stay in business. He wasn't in the mood "to feed all the bums and malcontents within our shores." He was of the view that FDR's cabinet had moved so far to the left that he might as well let the legendary muckraker "Upton Sinclair function in their place."

> It isn't the shrieking guy who never had anything, and who knows how to chisel in on the charity rackets that needs help more than the self-respecting business and professional man who has tried to attain a competence and live up to the best ideals of American citizenship, still trying to remain composed and cheerful with everything crashing about him. He is the consumer that pays and is being taxed to utter desperation to maintain the policies of the New Deal.[23] (Orrin [name illegible], Aug. 30, 1934)

Even if middle-class people could manage for the time being, just how long, they wanted to know, could they last if they had to support the costs of the New Deal? They saw themselves as alone in the maelstrom because the rich did not need anyone's help and the poor were soaking up all the government largesse. It was the middle class that was fast becoming an endangered species. "To date, we have not begged for government aid," wrote a Texas housewife.

> We have managed to stand on our own feet, but how long will we last? Our pride is in the dust, our hopes in shreds, what can we do? We worked hard, saved a little money, kept the law to the letter and where are we? . . . [I am] afraid for the middle class, caught and crushed between the upper class, whose wealth is sufficient protection for them and the lower class, whose helplessness, inefficiency and poverty give them government aid.[24] (Mrs. George Carsey, Dallas, Tex., May 26, 1934)

> I think your administration is the most inequitable this country has ever known. You pamper poverty and throttle thrift. The industrious,

Figure 1.1. Trends in the National Unemployment Rate, 1929–1940

Source: Robert Margo, "Employment and Unemployment in the 1930s," *Journal of Economic Perspectives* 7, no. 2 (1993): 41

■ Treating work relief recipients as unemployed
□ Treating work relief recipients as employed

1929 3.2%

1930 8.7%

1931 15.9%

1932 23.6%

1933 24.9%

1934 21.7% 16.0%

1935 20.1% 14.2%

1936 16.9% 9.9%

1937 14.3% 9.1%

1938 19.0% 12.5%

1939 17.2% 11.3%

1940 14.6% 9.5%

the frugal, the efficient are penalized to promote sloth, waste and incompetence. It is all wrong, unfair, unnatural. . . . Your administration has coddled those whom it was politically expedient to conciliate and imposed upon those who, like myself are politically unorganized although we probably pay more taxes in the aggregate and have a greater stake in the country than any other class.[25] (Irwin Spear, Boston, Mass., Feb. 10, 1936)

Why . . . don't you try to help me, and millions more like me, you are just helping part of the people. You give those fellows relief [who] never paid any tax to the government. People like me you hinder or make it harder all along. . . . You may put to work 7,000,000 people or more, but . . . you are [pushing] more than 7,000,000 down in the gutter further, with high sales tax on food stuff and higher taxes to meet.[26] (John Snyder, Geneva, Ind., Apr. 15, 1935)

Those who were persuaded that a national catastrophe called for unusual measures still worried that Roosevelt's intrusion was far too extensive. The government, they argued, was spending too much money on relief. As the Depression dragged on, with unemployment lines and breadlines wrapping around the block, ordinary Americans responded to some of the earliest national opinion polls that wanted to know whether they thought the government should reduce its spending on relief. The answer was a resounding yes, though somewhat more tempered when respondents were asked if the cuts should be leveled in their own community.

As figure 1.1 shows, unemployment levels fluctuated during this period, trending down from the peak of 24.9% in 1933 to about 9% in 1937 (depending on whether relief workers are included or not). When compared with the benchmark of 3.2% in 1929, the entire period was marked by catastrophic news in the labor market. The ranks of the dispossessed grew from the traditionally indigent to include a new kind of poor: formerly stable earners who differed "sharply from the chronically dependent relief population of the past" and instead represented a "mass of respectable, hard-working family men unable to find work," many of whom were from the ranks of white-collar occupations.[27]

Historian Michael Katz argues that the changing demography of the truly desperate encouraged the new poor to see their unemployment as a consequence of factors beyond their control rather than as evidence of character defects, and hence to feel that they had a right to demand a socialized remedy in the form of government relief.[28] Robert Bremner concurs: "The distinction Roosevelt and the New Deal made between the unemployed and the chronic dependents, and the special status accorded the 'employables,' made for a more favorable public attitude toward, and a better self-image among, the unemployed."[29] William Brock argues that with the removal of relief from local jurisdiction, where the most traditional and negative attitudes prevailed, to the comparatively more forgiving arena of the federal government, "silently but unmistakably" a more tolerant attitude emerged that "helped to transform public attitudes toward poverty":

> In 1932, when federal relief came to the top of the political agenda, the argument that prevailed was that it should not begin; in 1935, the most articulate criticism . . . was that it was being brought to an untimely end. . . . The wall between federal and local responsibility had been breached, and it would never be rebuilt again.[30]

Public opinion polls, which commenced in the midst of Roosevelt's first term, present a decidedly more mixed picture. In polls taken in 1935, 1937, and 1939, respondents were asked whether government should slash federal relief spending. Earlier polls imply a public desire to see federal relief spending cut, but these strong responses should be viewed with caution, because we are not able to adjust for potential sampling problems in these data.[31] In the later data, which we were able to weight in order to mitigate sampling errors, we see a sharply divided public—about half wanted to see relief spending slashed. Unemployment levels had fallen steadily but remained north of 10%, which meant that hundreds of thousands of American families were still reliant on federal relief for support.[32]

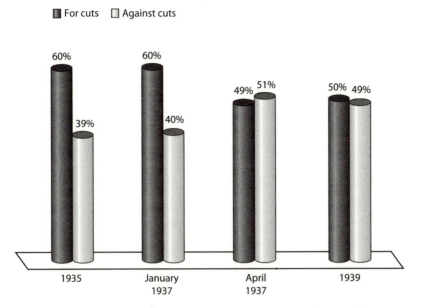

Figure 1.2. New Deal–Era Support for Cuts in Federal Relief Spending, 1935–1939
Note: The April 1937 and the 1939 data have been weighted to correct for any problems
due to sampling errors. The raw data are unavailable for the 1935 or the January 1937
sample; therefore the numbers presented are simple cross-tabulations as reported by Gallup. The difference between the weighted and unweighted numbers for the two weighted
samples suggests that support for relief was actually somewhat more substantial than the
non-weighted cross-tabulations imply, which should be taken into account when evaluat-
ing the unweighted data.
Source: Gallup

   In 1935, FDR dismantled the Federal Emergency Relief Administration (FERA), then only two years old, and began to transfer much
of the fiscal responsibility for relief for "unemployables" to the states
and localities, reserving federal support for public employment. Is
it possible the negative attitudes toward federal relief in this opinion poll are merely ratifying that decision? Unlikely. Though much
of the tab for general poor relief was shifted away from the federal
government, it was still very much in the "relief business" through
the matching funds it continued to provide for categorical programs
like Aid to Dependent Children (ADC, the forerunner of today's
"welfare") and Old Age Assistance (the ancestor of Supplemental

Security Income, or SSI). Moreover, it seems a bit far-fetched to imagine that the intricacies of intragovernment transfers were clear in the public mind.

After all, the modern welfare system is also primarily a state responsibility, but this is not widely recognized by the average American, who continues to hold consistently strong negative views about cash relief, regardless of which level of government is footing the bill. As we will see in chapter two, public dismay over mounting expenditures in the welfare system and the desire to see "federal expenditures" forced down continued unabated, even after a state-based system had been in place for decades. Finally, it seems implausible that as late as 1939, respondents to these polls were still fixated on policy decisions made four years earlier.

It is more likely that these critical attitudes were influenced by the relative improvements in the economy that preceded the major recession of 1937–38. The extreme poverty of the early Depression years helped break through traditional resistance to government support for the poor, but when conditions began to improve slightly, the "old belief that most paupers owed their misfortune to defects in character and could be justly treated according to the stringent principles of the old poor law" resurfaced.[33] The fact that the "unemployed councils" agitated for continuing poor relief and that marches for relief happened regularly did not move the general public to embrace the kind of welfare rights perspective that grew in popularity among activists thirty years later. It bears remembering that even in the depths of the Depression, when unemployment crested at 25%, 75% of the nation's workers were still on the job. We would like to think they were filled with sympathy for their hapless brethren, and no doubt many were. But it was not a universal sentiment.

Cuts were particularly appealing to those individuals and firms that were on the brink of collapse, for whom the additional tax burdens required to fuel the New Deal were the last straw:

Continually running the country further into debt, the constant threat of inflation, the encouragement of strikes[34] . . . the use of federal money in taking care of the unemployed (without telling the unemployed that this is an absolutely temporary measure and that they will have to use their own ingenuity in working out their own problems) can only bring this country to the brink of ruin.[35] (H. S. Adler, Chicago, Aug. 17, 1934)

The middle classes have suffered a great deal. Their homes are mortgaged and lost in many cases, their deposits gone, assessed for bank failure, dividends cut off, and being taxed to death, also out of work, yet they are supposed to keep the country together, support the schools and churches, and cannot remain [there] much longer. Many have already committed suicide. What has the government done to help this class? They do not belong to a union, so nothing has been done but to raise their taxes.[36] (J.A.R., businessman, New York City, no date)

Not only were the costs considered ruinous in the here and now, critics of FDR argued he was yoking the country to a millstone. "Just think what you are doing," wrote an exasperated John Moore of Greenfield, Ohio, in September 1934. "[You are] putting the burden of debt on generations to come for 1000 years to pay off the debt of a waste administrating money to some people whom never worked and will never work."[37]

The "Narcotic" of Relief

The best way on earth to ruin a person is to give him something for nothing and to encourage him not to work. I am 68 years old and am doing as much work as I ever did. . . . Your policies encourage people to be dependent, dishonest [and] deceitful. . . . If you only knew how your policies are wrecking the morals, integrity and character of the people.[38]
—William Snider, Dublin, Tex., Jan. 10, 1939

Public animosity toward "lazy" nonworkers, living the high life on a cash stipend, filled the popular press even as the same newspapers carried photographs of endless lines of job seekers queuing in front of the few firms that were hiring. In language reminiscent of Ronald

Reagan's "welfare-queen" anecdotes fifty years later, business leaders worried about the disappearance of the work ethic. "Many of the poor and lazy class do not want work," argued a New York businessman in 1936, "and they will not work if offered it."

> They go on relief and get adequate funds, so why work? It is alleged that some even got the Red Cross flour and then traded it for gas for their cars. To cut it all out will work hardship on some, but the rotten spots should be taken out at once.[39] (J.A.R., businessman, New York City, no date)

The business community was not the only group antagonistic toward relief. Farmers, who suffered massively during the Depression, also looked askance at those on public assistance, believing they were living the high life while the dreams of rural Americans withered on the vine. Resilient to the end, farming families made do with what they had and looked on those on relief as profligate. "The fall of prices at the close of the war took away our farm and savings," wrote one farmer's wife to the Committee on Economic Security.

> In spite of this, we have managed to send eight of our children through high school. . . . I know just what those people on relief must have as necessities and what are luxuries. How they could get along on half of what they do and still be healthy. How they could be clean even if they don't have money. Near us is a family on relief, the head of which claims he is entitled to help from the state because he was hurt on a state truck a year ago. But he was on relief then or he wouldn't have been there. Now he lives on his father-in-law's place, and while the sale of their produce came to more than my husband's wages, the relief truck delivers their groceries and fuel just the same while we had to spend all we could make, and all my children could give us, to live.[40] (Mrs. C. B., West McHenry, Ill., no date)

The more she scrimped and saved and pulled from the pay packets of her own children, the more she resented what she saw as the easy life of the family on the dole. And where was that comfort coming from? Her pocket!

> We still have a boy in school and a girl in the grades and my boy earned his school clothes, his books, and helped us pay rent all summer, while their children had vacations. They had money for every kind of ingestible food, while we went with only the necessities. They drove their car without a license, while we walked. They have medical care, even, and order the woman around for $44 worth of "vitality shots" while we had to wait until we got well when we were sick. Therefore, we and our children, trying to keep from relief, are taxed 3 cents on every dollar to keep these people who have all the things we cannot have, and when I complained to the authorities, they said, "Why, you haven't been refused relief, have you?" All of our children work, and not through luck. But if they have to give us everything they are being penalized for being industrious and are paying two sets of relief taxes—one for us and one for the neighbors who rest while the children work. We object to having "relievers" trying to put us on relief.[41]

No such reservations were expressed about the federal support flowing to the heartland courtesy of the Agricultural Adjustment Administration (AAA). The AAA was understood as a legitimate way to protect the family farm from the downward spiral of prices. But relief recipients were another matter, even when they were long-time neighbors who had lost their land.[42] Public assistance was regarded as a cesspool of corruption that would never cure poverty but instead would *cause* it:

> As it is carried on, [the relief program] is making paupers faster than any method ever devised. The relief roll has steadily increased since the new administration came into power. . . . The relief families are sure learning fast how to work the racket, and live better than the average farmer.[43] (Willard Davis, Dover-Foxcroft, Maine, Dec. 6, 1934)

Cash relief came in for particularly heavy criticism. It was the devil's work, threatening to sap the motivation of citizens, an attitude reinforced at the policy level by extremely meager stipends and harsh, overbearing forms of surveillance designed to make the experience of public assistance maximally unpleasant.[44] Work relief, public employment created to address unemployment, was far more acceptable.[45] Even the captains of industry (surveyed by *Fortune*) concurred with these policies: 74.5% of business leaders supported relief in the form of government-created jobs, while a mere 9% supported cash relief.[46]

FDR was no fan of cash relief either. In his second State of the Union address, delivered in January of 1937, he spoke directly to the issue, lamenting the impact of this form of "poor support" on the five million indigent Americans on public assistance:

A large proportion of these unemployed and their dependents have been forced on the relief rolls. The burden on the Federal Government has grown with great rapidity. We have here a human as well as an economic problem. When humane considerations are concerned, Americans give them precedence. The lessons of history, confirmed by the evidence immediately before me, show conclusively that continued dependence upon relief induces a spiritual and moral disintegration fundamentally destructive to the national fiber. To dole out relief in this way is to administer a narcotic, a subtle destroyer of the human spirit. It is inimical to the dictates of sound policy. It is in violation of the traditions of America. Work must be found for able-bodied but destitute workers. The Federal Government must and shall quit this business of relief.[47]

Roosevelt's primary concern was the prospect that the dole—or charity "baskets," demeaning public jobs like "cutting grass, raking leaves or picking up papers in public parks—would "sap the vitality of our people." The government, he argued, had to be in the business of doing more than just "preserving the bodies of the unemployed from destitution, but also their self respect, their self reliance, and courage and determination."

In this conviction, FDR was completely in line with what his own staff was telling him about the mood of the country. Reports from the Committee on Economic Security (CES) echoed the normative assumption that work was the measure of worth in American society. Cash relief—federal charity—was an insult to its recipients. "Socially, unemployment insurance is likewise both sound and just," argued CES staffer Alexander Holzoff:

> Obviously, from the standpoint of society, the pauperization and demoralization of a large proportion of the population resulting from their being dependent on charity, frequently inadequate, is highly undesirable. Equally it is unjust to the individuals concerned. There is something basically and fundamentally unjust and unfair to say to a person ready, able and willing to earn his living by the sweat of his brow, that there is no work for him to do, and he must stand in the bread-line in order to keep from starvation, or at best undergo the humiliation of going on the relief rolls.[48]

Written not long after the Depression came to an end, Donald Howard's detailed analysis of all major WPA programs noted that if cash relief was understood as getting "something for nothing," work relief was at least a reassurance to a skeptical public, including relief recipients themselves that the indigent were willing to labor for their wages.[49]

Ordinary people, whose attitudes were captured by Roper and Gallup in some of the earliest opinion polls, concurred: only certain kinds of generosity should be underwritten by the government as the instrument for protecting the common good, namely those that opened up opportunity to work.

The Roosevelt archives are filled with letters from people who hated the dole but favored public employment. Many of the letters we discuss here were written some time before the earliest opinion polls were available and provided the White House with an early warning of the gathering sentiment in the country at large, both among those who were managing without government help and

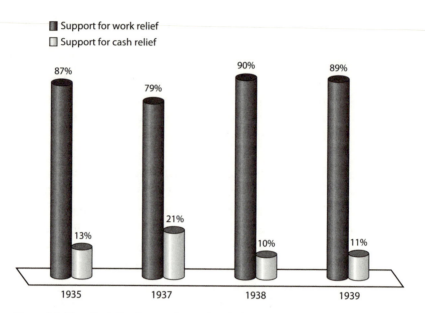

■ Support for work relief
☐ Support for cash relief

Figure 1.3. New Deal–Era Support for Work Relief versus Cash Relief, 1935–1939
Note: We were unable to create weights to correct for sampling error in the data presented, thus all results are subject to sampling error. However, the wide gap between support for work relief versus support for cash relief suggests that weights would do very little to change the general conclusion.
Source: Gallup

those who were desperate. Alvie Atkinson, a work relief administrator in Detroit, wrote to the president on behalf of two CWA employees to thank him for giving people work rather than unearned cash. [50] "It gives me undue pleasure to be the custodian and transmitter of such a message," Atkinson wrote," for it comes from the hearts of men who have been cast down deep in the mire of despair, and . . . it is a true expression from those whose hopes and courage are now rising on the wave of confidence resulting from the daring, conviction and action of your very good self, OUR PRESIDENT" (emphasis in original).[51]

Atkinson's view, that work was dignity, and restoring dignity was the most important task before the president, was embraced by many. Indeed, much of the sociological research on the impact of the Depression era focused on the crisis of the American family. From

Komarovsky's *The Unemployed Man and His Family* to Bakke's *The Unemployed Worker*, social analysts worried about the psychological deterioration of fathers denied the traditional role of breadwinner and the impact on families when mothers and teens assumed the role, since they were cheaper to employ and therefore more likely to find work.[52] Poverty was a serious problem that would hopefully subside in time, but the disintegration of character was potentially permanent. Public employment put (meager) money into the pockets of families; more important, it restored self-confidence and prevented a slide into irreversible alcoholism, despair, and suicide—problems that were all too real in the 1930s.

The Public Health Nurses of the Hygienic Institute in La Salle, Illinois, wrote to Roosevelt in December 1933 to commend him for recognizing the sociological disaster in the making. "Our community is made up largely of working people, many only one generation removed from Europe," they explained. "The state of mind they were in could not continue long without disaster. Through your work program you have brought confidence and hope to them and many are able to whistle and sing today for the first time in many, many months."[53]

Two representatives of the Resolution Committee of the Associated Societies of the Seventh Congressional district of Illinois agreed with these sentiments and wrote to FDR on behalf of their own members, who were small business owners and working men, home owners and pillars of the community.

> You our Dear and by all Beloved President [have] our deep gratitude. . . . You will overcome all the obstacles from wherever or whomever they may be to bring about our forgotten man, woman, and child, to give them the opportunity to earn an honest living not through charity but by useful and dignified employment in our much plentiful country.[54] (Adam [name illegible] and John Glab, Chicago, Nov. 30, 1933)

From far and wide, the embrace of work relief was strong and heartfelt:

A friend of mine, past middle age, who had aged ten years in the last three, walked up to me with a springy step, square shoulders and happy eyes. He had EARNED his first CWA paychecks and a new faith in the future. Your critics say we cannot SPEND our way to prosperity. I say you are spending nothing, you are re-creating the manhood of America.[55] (Robert [last name illegible], Racine, Wisc., Dec. 11, 1933; emphasis in original)

I have followed with grateful appreciation your unerring approach to the proposition that the dole per se is quote a subtle destroyer of the human spirit—that work must be found for able bodied but destitute workers—that we must preserve not only the bodies of the unemployed from destitute [destitution?] but also their self respect their self reliance and courage and determination unquote.[56] (Caleb Moore, New York City, Jan. 6, 1935)

[Work relief] is a wonderful opportunity to be of real service to our fellow men and in the work I am at present doing I feel it a wonderful thing I am with the playground relief taking care of the children while their parents attend school. . . . I am delighted to serve humanity in this field.[57] (Rovaida T. Murray, San Diego, Calif., Mar. 17, 1935)

We should not conclude from these letters, or from the polls that show a preference for work relief over the dole, that relief workers were thought of as completely legitimate. Not only was the brother's keeper sentiment limited to those who worked for their pay, those who found their jobs through the offices of public employment services were reminded daily of their second-class status. Seventy-nine percent of the respondents to a Gallup poll in 1940 said that WPA workers should not have the right to belong to a union; 85% thought they should not have the right to strike.[58] Seventy-three percent of Americans believed WPA workers should, as a matter of law, be paid less than workers in private industry.[59] Eighty-one percent of Americans receiving relief payments voiced support for a Pennsylvania law requiring relief recipients to accept any job offered to them by government, no matter what kind of job it was, on pain of losing all cash support.[60]

Some sectors of American opinion were allergic to work relief in any case. Small businessmen objected on the grounds that it undermined the upper hand they had held in the hiring halls. Roosevelt put in place a wage system that was to compensate WPA workers at the "prevailing wage" in the area. Mindful of the resistance he would face if he tried to fatten the pay packets of low-wage workers, particularly African Americans in the South, he countered with something close to parity, if less generous to unskilled workers than to those with blue- or white-collar skills. Employers often reacted with scorn, since what they wanted was to get the most work for the least expense. As one businessman wrote to the president, "No doubt there would have been a revolt if the poor had not been fed. However, like the other projects, there has been abuse in this too."

> Wages which have been paid are excessive, upsetting local employment conditions. Many, naturally, quit their jobs to get from 45 cents to $1.20 an hour from the government, and this aggravated the situation still more. Men, we are told, left the farms to join the relief.[61] (J.A.R., New York City, no date)

Animosity toward WPA projects was just about as strong as the disdain for the workers themselves.[62] A New York City businessman wrote to the popular radio personality Boake Carter to complain, "So much of this federal spending on worthless and ungainful projects it is tragic, and the people will have to pay with interest. Someone in the *Post* compared it with building the unprofitable pyramids."

Jason Scott Smith has made the point that attitudes toward Depression-era public works projects were greeted by a form of "reverse NIMBY-ism."[63] People were far more enthusiastic about public works that benefited their own communities than they were about projects that helped someone else, "over there." The prevailing view seems to have been inspired by something closer to "what's in it for me?" than the more admirable sentiments we remember as underlying the philosophy and practice of the New Deal.

Historians Linda Gordon and Lizbeth Cohen have both argued that attitudes about poverty changed during the Depression because, as Gordon explains, "poor people offered their interpretations of the problem through social and political activism that helped to redefine the causes of poverty and the criteria for who deserved help," an outburst of sentiment that "cohered to form a pro-welfare political culture."[64] This is certainly true in the case of social movement activists, who did indeed make their viewpoints known.

The trail of public opinion offers a more divided and fluctuating perspective, with majorities supporting cuts in federal relief expenditures, but substantial minorities leaning in the opposite direction. One thing the proponents and opponents shared, though, was a decided preference for work over cash relief.[65] If this is the definition of a pro-welfare political culture, in which public employment comes to be seen as a legitimate, if not entirely welcome, function of government, then the evolution these historians note is clear as well in the tracks of public opinion. Public employment was never accepted as equal in respect to worthiness to private sector work, but it was understood by millions to be a reasonable government response to an economic crisis. That said, it is far from a brother's keeper sentiment if by that we mean a civic obligation to care for all of our citizens, no matter how weak, no matter how unfortunate. This version of civic obligation means we help those willing to work. As we will see, this is a persistent theme in the national culture from the 1930s to the present.

SIDELINING THE TOWNSEND SOLDIERS

Of all the programs to emerge from the New Deal, Social Security is the one we consider most sacred even today. It is often deemed the "third rail" of social policy, and woe be unto the politician who touches it. New Deal–era polling data suggest that support for the elderly was relatively popular, particularly in comparison with other relief efforts. Just a few months before the implementation of the Social Security Act, the public was broadly enthusiastic about the idea of old-age insurance, with 68% supporting the "compulsory old age insurance plan" funded jointly by employers and workers.[66] Indeed, the basic idea of old-age insurance as framed by Roosevelt's Social Security program received consistent high marks from the public.[67] However, cash support for the elderly was more controversial than its contemporary legacy suggests. Social Security, with its joint responsibility shared among the worker, the employer, and government, was one model of several competing for public attention in the early years of the Great Depression. That Social Security won out over the competing models suggests the limits of public generosity, even in the darkest of economic times.

In 1934, one of the worst years of the Depression, a California physician named Francis Townsend called for a $200 monthly pension for each person over the age of sixty. The purpose of the Townsend Plan was threefold: it was supposed to support elderly Americans, relieve their adult children of the economic burden of their care, and stimulate demand by encouraging spending. Townsend pensions were to be financed by a 2% federal sales tax, and (somehow) the funds had to be spent every month.

Historians have suggested that the Townsend Plan received the enthusiastic support of elderly Americans across the country, many of whom had seen their savings and retirement incomes wiped out by the Depression.[68] Five thousand Townsend Clubs—which counted two million members—were established to promote regional and national conventions, known to many through their anthem "Onward Townsend Soldiers."[69] Yet the Townsendites failed to get their plan through. When one looks at the results of the 1936 Gallup poll on the subject, it is hardly surprising that the legislature failed to act. This is as close to total rejection as we ever see in the business of opinion polls.

The Social Security Act was passed by Congress in August 1935, four months before this poll was conducted. Was the overwhelming rejection of the Townsend Plan motivated by the recognition that the problem was already under control? That is perfectly plausible, but there are reasons to question such an interpretation. First, while Social Security was well regarded, the benefits it provided did not become available until 1942, six years into the future. Moreover, Social

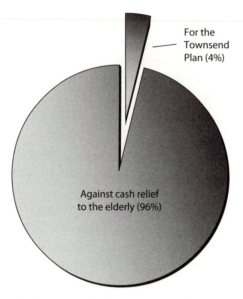

For the Townsend Plan (4%)

Against cash relief to the elderly (96%)

Figure 1.4. Support for the Townsend Plan to Pay Each Elderly Couple $200 a Month, January 1936

Note: Raw data are not available for this survey. The data are presented unweighted and thus are subject to sampling error. However, the margin by which respondents rejected the Townsend Plan provision suggests that weighting would be unlikely to change the overall conclusion.

Source: Gallup

Security payments were fairly modest: $20 a month as late as 1939. The common view at the time was that $40 a month was closer to a fair standard for the elderly.[70] As a consequence, the Townsend movement continued to push for higher benefits after Social Security had become the law of the land.

We should also bear in mind that in 1935, Social Security covered a large proportion of the American workforce, but it was still a minority. Eligibility rested on a number of criteria, including firm size (larger than ten) and sectoral membership. Workers had to be part of the "interstate commerce" system to be covered. Battles raged for decades after its inception over who was and who was not involved in interstate commerce. It was not until the 1950s that something approximating universal coverage for workers became a reality. (Nonworkers are still not covered except as widows of workers.) One might imagine a continuing degree of popular support for the Townsend Plan, given these worries about eligibility, benefit levels, and the onset of coverage, and no doubt its strongest adherents saw the matter in exactly these terms. Yet the national opinion polls ran in the other direction.

It is perhaps easier to understand the 1936 polling results when we remember how small the median income was in the 1930s. Townsend proposed giving the elderly the equivalent of $2,400 yearly at a time when the annual income of a full-time public school teacher was $1,227, that of an electrical worker was $1,550, and that of a college teacher was $3,111. Even Roosevelt's inner circle was down on the idea. Edwin Witte, president of the CES (and often called "the father of Social Security"), slammed the Townsend Plan in the press.[71]

Sociologist Ed Amenta, whose definitive study of the Townsend movement provides the best understanding of its contributions to the development of our welfare state, argues that it was indirectly responsible for the success of Social Security, in part because politicians could point to succeeding proposals as fiscally conservative alternatives.[72] Social Security was, from the very beginning, publicly described as "self-financing" and limited to the deserving workers, as opposed to a tax-eating pension system disbursed to any needy elder.[73] Though the system was highly redistributive, providing a much larger payoff to low-wage workers than to those who contributed more at the high end, those details largely escaped the public then (and now). Instead, it appeared to be a universal program that made uniform demands on workers and provided benefits to all of them. FDR's policy gurus were particularly keen to distinguish Social Security from a European-style social insurance system. It was to be an American plan, with an American reliance on employment, rather than an "all-sufficient program for economic security."[74]

The Townsend Plan proposed a universal entitlement for the elderly, not a conditional program for retired workers. In this regard, what Townsend had in mind was more European in style, and was denounced for exactly this reason. Samuel Crowther, an economist active in the anti-pension movement, argued that "there are young bums as well as old bums, and neither has any claim whatsoever on society." The anti-pension activists denounced the Townsend Plan and other movements to create a national pension system as extremist, the "entering wedge of socialism."[75] Despite the head of steam the Townsend soldiers generated among the plan's devoted followers, by the 1950s it was politically irrelevant.[76] As Amenta makes clear, its legacy lies more in the increase in benefit levels for Social Security recipients than in anything else.

The architects of America's retirement system organized their thinking around the rights of workers, not the obligations of citizens for the elderly or the indigent. Social Security was not a brother's keeper concept; it was an insurance plan for workers. There were, however, exceptions to this somewhat puritanical orientation, including Old Age Assistance, which provided poor, elderly Americans with a small cash stipend regardless of their work history. Old Age Assistance was the largest cash relief program of the time and was quite popular, repeatedly receiving approval ratings of 90% or greater in Gallup polls conducted during the mid- and late 1930s.

One reason for the popularity of Old Age Assistance in the absence of a direct tie to recipients' work history may be the fact that Social Security's old-age work-based contributory framework did nothing to help those who had worked their entire lives but were too poor to manage and too old to return to the labor market. For these individuals, Old Age Assistance was a lifeline at a time when their working-age children were likely struggling to get by and therefore unable to offer much in the form of private aid. A second explanation is the persistent sympathy for various "deserving" groups in America. The belief that both children and the elderly deserve more of society's good will than the able-bodied, working-age adult who stands outside the labor market is a thread that runs throughout American social history.

As Linda Gordon and others have pointed out, "the Social Security Act created the contemporary meaning of 'welfare' by setting up a stratified system of provision in which the social insurance programs were superior both in payments and in reputation, while public assistance was inferior . . . [and] deeply stigmatized."[77] Nonworkers were dumped into Old Age Assistance, the "poor man's social security," ADC, the meager cash relief programs that survived the Depression, and the charitable agencies, which did what they could.

VARIATION AND CONSISTENCY IN ATTITUDES

Were Americans in communities hardest hit by the Depression more sympathetic to the poor and more supportive of government support for them? Or did they detest relief, regardless of how serious the unemployment statistics were in their states? Here we examine the relationship between the level of economic distress, race, region, and gender as they influenced support for government cutbacks in relief spending or the extent to which respondents thought it would be easy for those eliminated from the relief roles to find new jobs.

Regional Sympathies

Respondents in the east-central part of the country—Ohio, Michigan, Indiana, and Illinois—were significantly more likely than those in other parts of the country to support cuts in relief spending, as were respondents in the southern states. The findings from the South are perhaps less surprising, since the region was known for its conservatism and its legislators in Washington were among the most vociferous opponents of the New Deal. The east-central states are perhaps more surprising, since these are the areas that would eventually become industrial union strongholds, typically believed to be more supportive of New Deal policies that favored workers and strengthened unions' power (table 1.1).

We might imagine that in regions with higher unemployment we would see greater understanding of and sympathy for the plight of the unemployed. It is certainly the case that the unemployed themselves and unskilled workers (the most likely to be let go) were favorably disposed toward relief.[78] But in regions where they were more numerous, sympathy toward their plight was noticeably less vigorous than in regions with fewer employment problems. Respondents in high-unemployment states favored cutting both federal and

Table 1.1   Attitudes toward Relief by Individual Demographic Characteristics, 1936

	% Approving of Government Cuts in Relief Spending	% Agreeing Relief Spending Should Be Cut in Own Community	% Agreeing Persons Taken off Relief Jobs Will Easily Find Work
Region			
New England	51.3	37.9	17.8
Mid-Atlantic	55.1	51.0	22.8
East Central	70.8	64.9	40.7
West Central	55.9	46.9	14.8
South	61.5	50.3	24.4
Rocky Mountains	58.6	56.3	13.3
Pacific	51.2	45.4	16.6
Gender			
Men	60.9	54.3	24.7
Women	58.1	49.4	24.1
Age			
17–20 years	65.1	61.0	26.5
21–24 years	53.6	43.7	30.1
25–34 years	59.6	51.4	23.5
35–44 years	57.0	49.2	23.8
45–54 years	59.8	52.3	26.3
55 years and over	61.3	55.1	21.5
Occupation			
Professional	78.9	66.2	31.6
Business	73.1	64.9	36.0
Skilled Worker	61.6	54.8	24.9
Unskilled Worker	44.5	39.3	19.1
Unemployed	23.2	17.4	8.8
Race			
White	60.0	52.2	24.8
Non-white	36.0	35.0	4.3

Note: Data are weighted to correct for sampling error.
Source: Data are from Gallup. N = 2662.

local spending on relief, perhaps because the fiscal consequences of mass migration to the relief rolls was more salient and threatening there than in states with lower unemployment.

Historian James Patterson notes a downturn in popular sympathy for the poor by the latter part of the 1930s, as the public began expressing concern that relief programs were creating a new, permanently dependent pauper class of people who loafed on the jobs they were provided and avoided going off relief even when they could.[79] The visibility of work relief recipients in those states may well have stoked the resentment Patterson describes.

We sometimes forget that the Depression hit only sixty-five years after the end of the Civil War. Divisions between North and South were not fully healed, and the letters to Roosevelt reflect lingering regional antagonisms and the conviction, fully shared by FDR and his Brain Trust, that the South was an economic millstone around the nation's neck, sorely in need of reform.[80] Racial stereotypes were mixed in with anti-southern sentiment in a toxic brew that complained loudly about the willingness of minorities to take advantage of the system. "Southern 'colored people' are all able to work," explained Mr. J.R.R. McEwen, from Mountain Lakes, New Jersey. "But they seem to be just naturally lazy. . . .

> This country was built on hard work, and people were proud of their work, but nowadays they want to do the least possible, and if they can get it for nothing. . . . We in the North work harder and pay the most taxes.[81] (Sept. 15, 1935)

> Sure every d— nigger is for you—they never had it so easy—just lay around and live on northern money. Sure every foreigner is for you—[they are] <u>unnaturalized</u> and on <u>relief</u>.[82] (George Davis, [no place], Oct. 1, 1936; emphasis in original)

Race and Exclusion

African Americans were unable to access many of the benefits that flowed from the New Deal because they were subject to occupational exclusions that restricted their access to its main benefit programs.[83] As political scientist Ira Katznelson notes, farm workers and maids constituted 60% of the black labor force in the 1930s and nearly 75% of those who were employed in the South. All of them were "excluded from the legislation that created modern unions, from laws that set minimum wages and regulated the hours of work, and from Social Security until the 1950s."[84] In later years, the benefits of the GI Bill, particularly those that provided educational and mortgage assistance, were denied to black veterans either because they lived in neighborhoods deemed too risky for VHA loans or because the administration of educational benefits left them at the mercy of local decision makers, who were free to discriminate. Congruent with Martin Gilens's findings for the late twentieth century, our analysis confirms that states with higher percentages of nonwhites in the 1930s also were more likely to favor spending cuts, but only at the federal level (the slight preference for cuts at the local level is not statistically significant).[85]

As Jill Quagdagno's historical sociology of the American welfare state makes clear, these features of "progressive" legislation emerged out of a compromise between southern legislators, who promised to veto the entire package of New Deal reforms, and the Roosevelt administration, which was trying to preserve the maximum benefits for those it could help.[86] Hence, although we remember the New Deal (and later the GI Bill) as federal programs that, in the words of President Clinton, "raised the entire nation to a plateau of social well-being never before experienced in U.S. history," the reality was more complex. It laid a foundation for occupational mobility and personal wealth underneath native-born citizens, nonagricultural workers (including African Americans, though not very many), and veterans who lived in places with nondiscriminatory benefit administrators. This was but a fraction of the country's minorities.

In the 1930s, though, public opinion ran somewhat contrary to public policy. Democrats and Republicans across all regions and in all social classes rejected by a wide margin the main forms of occupational exclusion for every year that we have data. Even in the South, a region whose senators were more responsible than anyone else for the elimination of black labor from the protections of the Fair Labor Standards Act and Social Security, popular sentiment ran more than two to one in favor of extending Social Security coverage to farmworkers, household help, and "sailors," members of the mer-

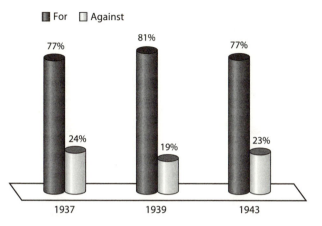

Figure 1.5. Early Support for Expanding Social Security Eligibility to Include Household Help, Sailors, and Domestic Workers, 1937–1943
Note: All data have been weighted to adjust for sampling error.
Source: Gallup

chant marine, a large and transient labor force responsible for most international shipping in the age before air transport. These findings suggest that what southern elites wanted dominated the legislation that emerged. Ordinary Americans who responded to the opinion polls on occupational restrictions did not concur. For them, the deserving were fundamentally defined by the broad category of private sector workers.

Alien and Undeserving

Immigrants and aliens came in for at least as powerful a drubbing,[87] a sentiment not unique to our own era.[88] "Aliens on relief" were met with open hostility.[89] In 1935, 67% of Americans agreed that they "should be returned to their own countries."[90] Two years later, 61% agreed that "people on relief who are not citizens of the United States or who have not yet applied for citizenship should be sent out of the country."[91] In 1939, 70% of Americans believed that "needy people living in this country who are not citizens and have not applied for citizenship" should not be given relief.[92]

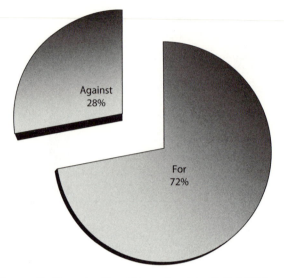

Figure 1.6. Support for Deporting Non-Citizens Receiving Relief, 1935
Note: Raw data are not available for this survey. The data are presented unweighted and thus are subject to sampling error. However, the margin by which respondents supported the deportation of non-citizens suggests that weighting the data would not change the substantive conclusion.
Source: Gallup

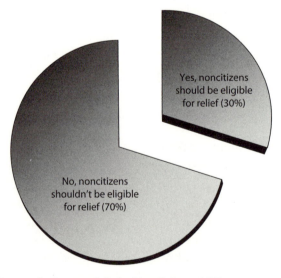

Figure 1.7. Support for Denying Relief to Non-Citizens, 1939
Note: Data are weighted to correct for sampling errors.
Source: Gallup

Yet, oddly enough, our analysis shows that states that had a greater proportion of non-citizen residents were *more* supportive of relief, and were less likely to support cuts in spending, than states that had fewer immigrants/aliens (table 1.2). Respondents might not have wanted immigrants to claim federal paychecks or handouts, but in areas with lots of them, support for federal largesse in general was not lacking. This hardly means that resident aliens were embraced, only that they were not the subject of greater hostility in the regions where they were more concentrated. That said, the whole country was inhospitable to the foreign-born and became even more so as the Depression deepened. Aliens were rejected not only because they undercut the wages of American workers but also because, in the view of some of Roosevelt's correspondents, they would support the federal machine that provided them with patronage jobs and rob the legitimate voter of the power to discipline FDR and his minions. "Has it occurred to you that millions not on relief who refuse to bend the knee and humbly obey the dicta you hand down?" asked Mr. J. Robert Smith of West Hempstead, Long Island.

> Do you recall the fate of that great "purger" of the French Revolution, Robespierre? Well, the voters of these United States still possess the right to change the complexion of Congress every two years and can politically "purge" most effectively. We mean to do this without the aid of bought Negro reliefers, WPA-ers, subsidized non-producers, pampered Alien and Labor Union hangers-on, or that misguided coterie surrounding you who have so amiably and so senselessly squandered our billions. We prefer to link up with the yearly increment of American-born new voters who will remember their heritage and keep it clean.[93] (Aug. 15, 1938)

Threatening Roosevelt's hold on power was a favorite (if ineffectual) pastime of many writers angry over the ability of other, less deserving voters to sway the course of elections. It was the middle class, they asserted, that should write the course of history:

It is the middle class in our country which elects a president. Not that of the ultra wealthy or moron class. Nevertheless it is with but few exceptions that we are getting a raw deal. The Moron, the lazy and the natural pan-handler is profiting thru crackpot and confiscatory legislation. If it is this class to which you refer as the forgotten

Table 1.2 State Attitudes toward Relief, as Predicted by State Demographics and Economic Characteristics (ßs)

	Mean % of State Approving of Cuts in Relief Spending	Mean % of State Agreeing That Relief Spending Should Be Cut in Own Community	Mean % of State Agreeing That Persons Taken off Relief Jobs Will Have Hard Time Finding Work
Household Type			
% Farm Households	−0.04 (−0.03)	0.12 *** (−0.04)	0.59 *** (−0.03)
% Homeowners	0.37 *** (−0.06)	0.10 ** (−0.04)	0.02 (−0.04)
Mean Home Value	0.00 *** (0.00)	0.00 *** (0.00)	0.00 *** (0.00)
Race and Citizenship			
% Non-White	0.40 *** (−0.03)	0.25 *** (−0.04)	−0.29 *** (−0.03)
% Non-Citizen	−0.70 *** (−0.08)	−1.43 *** (−0.09)	1.24 *** (−0.09)
Economics			
% Unemployed	1.86 *** (−0.27)	2.67 *** (−0.29)	−1.66 *** (−0.27)
Mean Income	−0.40 ** (−0.18)	0.16 (−0.20)	1.59 *** (−0.19)

Notes: Coefficients are ßs from OLS regressions that include all independent variables as predictors.
Standard errors in (parentheses): * significant at 10%; ** significant at 5%; *** significant at 1%.
Data are weighted to correct for sampling error.
Source: Data are from Gallup Poll #1936-0060 and from the authors' calculations based on the 1930 United States
Census Microdata (IPUMS 1930). N = 2659.

man, they first became so by forgetting themselves and their responsibilities.[94] (Leon Brown, Niantic, Conn., Oct. 31, 1934)

In the 1930s, the American middle class—defined as white-collar
or managerial employees, college educated, home-owning, or virtually any other reasonable metric by popular standards—was a very
small group. They were outnumbered and outvoted by the industrial
working class and rural Americans. Nonetheless, the idea that the
middle class was the honorable core of American culture had some
symbolic traction, even if it lacked clout.

It is perhaps understandable that public opinion toward non-
citizens on the dole would be negative.[95] But the hostility extended to
workers as well, even as unemployment fell in the wake of war time
shortages. "My travels take me all over this country," a listener wrote
to Boake Carter. "Here and in the Middle West I find many foreign-
ers, who are not American citizens and who do not pay taxes, holding
down good jobs." He continued,

> They do not vote. Not far from here, a friend of mine who has
> been "checking up" finds foreigners—many of them—on our relief
> rolls. This is very unfair. Those persons should be taxed heavily, or,
> better still, sent to their foreign homes.[96] (W.H.M., archaeologist,
> Phillips Academy, Andover, Mass., 1934)

> I am an old man, a factory worker in one of our largest furniture
> factories and one of the first ever to make furniture in America. The
> company started, more than seventy years ago, the policy of keeping
> all of its old help. Many of them are foreign born, but many of them
> have refused to become naturalized citizens. During our annual wel-
> fare and Red Cross drives, this element of foreign extraction refused
> bluntly and decisively to give one cent to charity to aid the poor of our
> city. Many of them are well-to-do, but let them be laid off for a day
> or two and they are the first to ask for help without a blush. Those
> that pay toward the welfare have to take care of these grafters.[97]
> (F.W.H., furniture factory worker, Grand Rapids, Mich., 1935)

Roosevelt got an earful along the same lines:

> We have in this country a great number of unemployed, likewise
> a great number of aliens, here legally and illegally. It is a particu-
> lar fact that from personal observation, I find that these aliens are
> in most cases employed . . . Immigrants today are competitors in
> all lines of work and business with our citizens and are the source
> of most of the communistic activity and crime. . . . I believe and
> recommend that immigration should be restricted, for a period at
> least.[98] (P. A. Adams, Portland, Ore., Feb. 16, 1935)

A 1942 National Opinion Research Center (NORC) survey confirmed these anecdotes: 79% of Americans believed that "people
working where [the respondent][99] was working should have to be citizens."[100] Sixty-six percent of Americans believed all workers in war
industries should be U.S. citizens.[101]

Mexican migrants were targeted with particular zeal.[102] In coop-
eration with the Mexican government, between 1929 and 1931 au-
thorities in the United States undertook the mass repatriation of
Mexican immigrants and their American-born children. Most came
from the Southwest (especially Texas and California), but the upper
Midwestern states also sent thousands of Mexicans "home" as well.[103]
In Los Angeles County, federal immigration officials and the federal
Emergency Committee for Employment chartered special trains to
send Mexicans and Mexican Americans south of the border.

The Roosevelt archives include many letters that implore the president to take action of just this kind. Ejecting the foreign-born would
go a long way toward curing unemployment and raising wages, he
was reminded. "Mexicans and Canadian aliens have been swarming
into California for several years as 'visitors,'" remarked L. R. Atkins
from the border town of San Diego, California.

> They immediately secure work in preference to American Citi-
> zens for this important reason: the average employer will employ
> aliens because they will for half of what an American citizen calls a

living wage. . . . [T]he un-employment question will not be solved unless Immigration is closed down for a number of years and all aliens deported and a "red-blooded he-man" replace that "ping-pong player" Miss Perkins as the Secretary of Labor.[104] (June 15, 1934)

GENDERING THE NEW DEAL

Alice Kessler-Harris, Linda Gordon, Gwendolyn Mink, and Theda Skocpol, among others, have written on the gendered nature of the welfare state.[105] By tying benefits such as old-age pensions and un-employment benefits to jobs, the New Deal "affirmed the status of recipients as independent and upstanding citizens and delineated the secondary position of those without good jobs or any at all."[106] Those without "good jobs" included transients; those without jobs at all were overwhelmingly women.

While the New Deal provided cash relief for some women— mother's pensions and widows' allowances, for example—others were completely excluded.[107] Never-married women with and without children or parents to support, divorced, or deserted women heads-of-household, and intact African American and other poor families whose male heads could not find jobs or earn sufficient wages to support their families were excluded from economic citizenship. Indeed, the draft language of the Full Employment Act denied women the right to earn a living, as Americans with "full-time housekeeping responsibilities" were explicitly excluded from the act's promise of "sufficient employment opportunities." [108]

Although women themselves were far more "relief friendly"—that is, less likely than men to favor reducing relief spending at either the federal or the local level—their generosity was not reciprocated. Public opinion was squarely behind exclusions based on gender. Gallup polls completed in 1936 and 1938 and Roper polls conducted in the 1940s show consistent public endorsement of the notion that married women should not work if their husbands could support them. As is well known, the unemployment levels of married men during the

Depression and after demobilization of the troops at the conclusion of the Second World War spawned a "women out of the workplace" movement and a surge of domesticity.

Antagonism toward working women did not derive from a general hostility to women. Indeed, when it came to protecting mothers—as opposed to female workers—Americans were inclined to be generous. For example, the public overwhelmingly supported the idea that

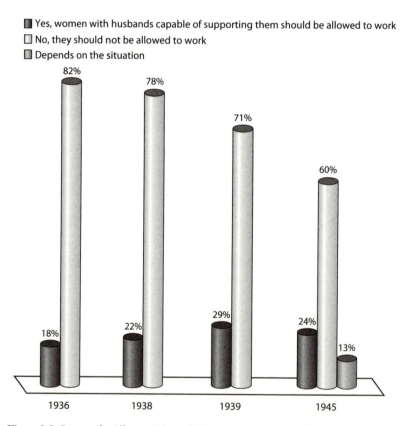

Figure 1.8. Support for Allowing Married Women to Join the Workforce, 1936–1945
Note: The 1939 data have been weighted to adjust for sampling error. Raw data are unavailable for 1936, 1938, and 1945; therefore, the numbers presented are simple crosstabulations as reported by Gallup. Weighting had no significant impact on the 1939 results, which suggests that sampling error is not driving the findings.
Source: Gallup

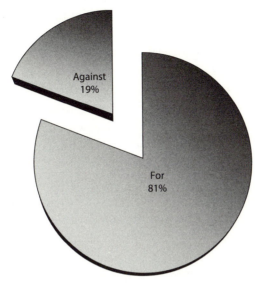

Figure 1.9. Support for Giving Mothers Government-Provided Medical Care at Childbirth, 1937
Note: Raw data are not available for this survey. The data are presented unweighted and thus are subject to sampling error. However, the margin by which respondents support government-provided medical care for new mothers suggests that weighting the data would not change the substantive conclusion.
Source: Gallup

pregnant mothers should receive medical care. But mothers as workers were no more welcome than illegal aliens.

THE LEGACY OF INCLUSION

While we have drawn attention to the public's restrictive definition of the common good, we must also note that the progressive character of the New Deal, flawed as it may appear from a contemporary vantage point, was remarkably expansive for its time. The idea that ordinary working men were entitled to a limited workday, that private sector workers had a right to seek union representation, that men who lost their jobs should be insured against the loss of income, that the government had a responsibility to provide public employment, that the right to unionize had to be protected, and that an insurance system should shield workers from poverty in their sunset years was a remarkable accomplishment.

The last act of the New Deal, the Servicemen's Readjustment Act of 1944 (otherwise known as the GI Bill), created an entitlement to a college education at government expense and low-cost mortgages underwritten by federal funds. These were unprecedented opportunities for working-class white men, who would have had far less hope of either higher education or home ownership before its provisions took effect.[109]

We should not minimize these accomplishments. They do represent an expanded commitment to civic inclusion. At the same time, the boundaries erected around the safety net in the 1930s and the mobility-enhancing policies of the 1940s were real enough. The "body civic" was a restricted set of people, defined by work status, birthplace, race, and gender. If this were just an outcome of policy decisions that were somehow enacted without the approval, tacit or explicit, of ordinary Americans, we could chalk this up to elite interests and legislative compromise. Public opinion data tell us otherwise. With some exceptions, public sentiment was often harsh toward the poor, and the public's sympathies were limited to those who could be put to work.[110] Those who found work courtesy of the government were not to be accorded equal respect or rights.

Why was FDR returned to office four times if the public was so divided over civic responsibilities toward the indigent? The president never camouflaged what he stood for or what he intended to do. He openly campaigned on a platform of wealth redistribution—especially in 1936, with his "soak the rich" tax—and his track record of unprecedented federal intervention into the realm of private enterprise. His efforts to increase government support for the poor were hardly a secret.

First, we must recognize that public opposition crystallized mainly around funding for "relief," which was popularly understood to mean cash handouts to the able-bodied could-be worker. This was never a winning strategy, since the public consistently believed that the indigent were malingering, could find work if they really wanted to, and didn't deserve the hard-earned tax dollars of the 75% of the country that was still employed and facing eroding wages. Roosevelt himself shared the public's distaste for cash relief and put more resources into public employment to cure poverty than any president before or since. While the president had more respect for the status and rights of WPA workers than the general public, he met his constituents halfway by emphasizing work over cash, even when the latter was cheaper to administer. And they responded favorably to this policy direction.

Indeed, given the consistency of public support for work over cash welfare, a theme we will meet again in the next chapter, we might ask instead why in ensuing decades, federal job creation efforts were all but abandoned.[111] Unless we want to think of the Second World War and subsequent conflicts that swelled the ranks of the military (public workers by another name), it has taken a downturn of the dimensions confronted by the Obama administration to revive much interest in New Deal–style public employment as a remedy for deep recession.

Some of the credit for FDR's policies surely belongs to the social movements and interest groups that pressured the White House and Congress throughout the Depression era. Perhaps the most famous of these was the Bonus Army, which represented veterans of the First World War who were not yet eligible for their pensions. In May 1932, 17,000 veterans traveled across the country from Portland, Oregon, to Washington, D.C., under the banner of the "Bonus Expeditionary Force," and camped out on the doorstep of Congress, demanding that the funds promised to them in 1924 be paid immediately, not in 1945 as originally scheduled. The House of Representatives capitulated to their demands, but the Senate refused, and the plan went down to defeat just in time to see several thousand disgruntled veterans riot. The spectacle of General Douglas MacArthur ordering federal troops to attack these aging veterans left an indelible public impression.

Organized labor, leaders of minority groups, and local government officials steadily and forcefully lobbied FDR. The Communist Party, then an active political force, sponsored marches and picketed local relief offices. Pressure groups were everywhere; some of them wrote the letters we have quoted in this chapter. In our own time, every decimal place of public opinion is calibrated, and even ordinary citizens are familiar with the idea of the "margin of error" in polling data. But in the 1930s and early 1940s, when the science of public opinion was in its infancy, it is reasonable to assume a more significant influence deriving from social movements than we might credit today. Public opinion was not irrelevant, but it did not receive the kind of popular treatment that we know all too well today. To the extent that FDR's policies evolved in favor of the interests of pressure groups, he was able to garner support at the ballot box.

Christopher Achen and Larry Bartels offer a different answer to the question of Roosevelt's electoral success.[112] They argue that there was no dramatic ideological shift during the Depression in favor of FDR's policies. We remember the era for its pathbreaking legislation and infer from it a dramatic reorientation of the American political mindset. Instead, they suggest that "short-term income gains and losses . . . cumulated willy-nilly into a durable Democratic majority in the electorate." In essence, those in office felt the electoral bite when bad economic news landed on their heads and they were tossed out, regardless of their ideological priors.

Looking around the world that was the 1930s, Achen and Bartels show that voters ejected "whoever was in office at the time" in Britain, Austria, Sweden, Canada, Ireland, and Weimar Germany. Collectively these governments represented political stripes ranging from liberal to conservative, even reactionary. Those that presided over economic recoveries were returned to office; those unlucky enough to oversee continuous recessions were tossed out. This model suggests that voters were looking for "what worked," and that the economic recovery that developed between 1933 and 1937 was perhaps more responsible for Roosevelt's lasting popularity than was a dramatic shift in the depth of the social contract. This would help to account for Roosevelt's narrower election victories in 1940 and 1944. If the sea change had been so thoroughgoing, we might have expected him to repeat the cakewalk of 1936, when FDR won more than 60% of the vote.[113] His victory was decisive but not as commanding as his earlier triumphs.

While there is much to commend the Achen-Bartels argument, it is also important to note that FDR attained a degree of secular sainthood that has never been matched by any other American president. Whatever the public opinion polls tell us about reservations over New Deal policies, one cannot ignore the role that deep and abiding affection for and gratitude toward the man played in his electoral victories. It is quite possible that his 1936 victory was guaranteed by the *realpolitik* that followed from the improvement in the economy. His next three victories, although achieved by smaller margins, represented the force of his public image and the confidence the public had in this hero, even when there was discontent with some of his policies.

Indeed, Roosevelt possessed those qualities of leadership that enabled him to sustain the momentum for the creation of the modern welfare state despite a public that could be surprisingly mean-spirited toward those who were down and out. To be sure, he curtailed aspects of the original New Deal in deference to those sentiments. And he maintained work relief even as many balanced-budget enthusiasts argued that cuts were needed or cash relief should be substituted because it was cheaper. FDR was no slave to public opinion but instead was a leader, if one with one eye on his detractors.

Whatever conclusion we might reach about the reasons for FDR's remarkable and durable staying power, the country as a whole was ambivalent about what was owed to its weakest and most vulnerable citizens. Even in our darkest hours, Americans did not share the sentiments of their European cousins, who were busy constructing far more generous welfare states based on citizenship rather than work status. If the findings of the opinion polls from 1935 onward and the letters to the White House for periods before and after can be taken as snapshots of American attitudes of the time, it was a variant of "helping those who help themselves," and even that was tempered by the conviction that the sooner the state retired from this role, the better.

2 Warring over the War on Poverty

Even the most inspired political speeches of our own time pale in comparison to the grace and power of Lyndon Johnson's landmark addresses on the Great Society. Though Johnson is remembered more for the debacle that was Vietnam, his secular sermons on the eradication of poverty are every bit as stirring as those of Roosevelt or Martin Luther King Jr. The specter of racial inequality and destitution in the midst of prosperity undercut American claims to moral superiority during the cold war. A nation of unparalleled wealth could not face the world, particularly not the world behind the Iron Curtain, without acknowledging the stark divisions that the Reverend King, Bobby Kennedy, and Michael Harrington brought to public attention.

The Great Society attempted to enable the nation's dispossessed to access the skills they needed to compete in the marketplace, and it knocked down discriminatory barriers to education, job markets, and political participation.[1] Poor health, a product of poverty exacerbated by inadequate medical care, had to be redressed, and Medicaid for the poor and Medicare for retirees were both part of the package.

Bold as it was, though, the War on Poverty did not fundamentally attack the structure of inequality; it was not an income redistribution scheme but rather an investment in "human capital." As historian Michael Katz and others have argued, Johnson sought to provide the toolkit individuals needed to compete, but he did not ask society to rearrange the economic hierarchies that created poverty in the first place.[2]

Richard Nixon is remembered neither for his oratory nor for his commitment to redressing the problem of poverty. Yet Nixon's domestic policy legacy is more important than we often credit. As historian Joshua Freeman has noted, federal social spending, adjusted for inflation, rose at an annual rate of nearly 10% under Nixon, compared to just under 8% during the Kennedy-Johnson years. For this reason, Freeman suggests, "the Nixon administration represented the last great moment of liberal rule."[3] The centerpiece of his domestic policy, the Family Assistance Plan (FAP), which was closer to a Nordic-style income subsidy program than anything we have seen since, was a critical contribution. While the FAP failed to win the approval of Congress and was never passed into law, other legislative victories indirectly inspired by the plan, including the Earned Income Tax Credit, have become effective instruments for attacking poverty at the federal level.

Neither Johnson nor Nixon was led to these ideas by a huge public push for reform. Of course, loud voices in the political choir urged action on racial injustice and economic inequality. Civil rights leaders dogged Johnson's heels and urged the president to be proactive, arguing that programs providing economic opportunity and human capital investment would help to realize racial equality. Indeed, though celebrated for his determined leadership of the civil rights movement, Martin Luther King Jr. was as committed to economic justice throughout his life as he was to any other principle. In 1972, George McGovern leaned on Nixon from the left with his own proposal for a guaranteed minimum income, a "demogrant" that would have given every American $1,000 annually, regardless of their work status.

Spurred by the growing unrest in the nation's largest cities, these political elites were pushing the federal government to address economic inequality and racial discrimination. But there is scarce evidence that they had a public wind at their backs either for the War on Poverty or for the FAP. Sociologists Clem Brooks and Jeff Manza have made the point that public opinion is essential to sustain a major social program, but the original impetus for these landmark pieces of social policy cannot really be chalked up to such a groundswell.[4]

Once launched, Great Society programs aimed at developing human capital enjoyed relatively high levels of popular support.

For example, the Jobs Corps and Head Start programs were rated the "most effective" in a 1967 survey asking respondents to rank Great Society programs.[5] But it's not as if Johnson identified *public* concern over the educational problems of poor children or the employment gaps among minority youth and then sought to remedy them. Instead, LBJ walked into something of a vacuum in the public mind where poverty was concerned and inserted some progressive ideas precisely where he believed they could do the most good.

That opinion vacuum was not total, though. The public did have some ideas about what was appropriate as an arena of government action and what was not, and its reservations reflect the continuing limitations that became evident during FDR's time. For example, support for universal access to employment was weak during the Great Society. The National Election Studies (NES) asked some version of this question from the late 1950s through the late 1960s: "The government in Washington ought to see to it that everybody who wants to work can find a job." In 1960, 59% believed that government ought to see to it that every person had a good job. By 1964, that figure was down to only 31%, where it remained in 1968. Americans were increasingly likely to agree that "government ought to just let people get ahead on their own." In 1960, only 24% offered this response. By 1964, 43% wanted government to leave people alone, and by 1968, 48% held this opinion.

One of the lasting achievements of the Great Society, the creation of Medicare and Medicaid, was also accomplished despite tepid public support for guaranteed access to affordable health care. Between 1956 and 1968, the NES asked some version of this question: "The government ought to help people get doctors and hospital care at low cost." Support for this premise peaked in 1962, when 62% of all Americans agreed. By 1964, when Johnson was hard at work putting health insurance for the poor and the elderly into law, overall support had dwindled to 50%. While some would argue that this is a large figure, the tide of public opinion was moving in the wrong direction for the president's initiatives. Even among Democrats, who were typically far more supportive of Johnson's Great Society objectives than Republicans, support for a government-backed health in-

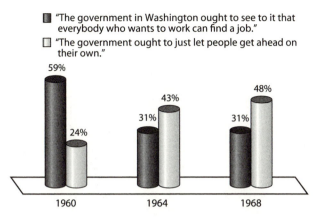

■ "The government in Washington ought to see to it that everybody who wants to work can find a job."

☐ "The government ought to just let people get ahead on their own."

Figure 2.1. Support for Government-Guaranteed Jobs, 1960–1968
Source: National Election Studies

surance scheme for the poor was losing ground. The trajectory of public opinion was not encouraging from the perspective of those who believed in LBJ's objectives.

Moreover, public support for a Medicare-style program diminished over the same period of time that Johnson worked to enact his capstone accomplishments. In March 1962, 55% of those surveyed by Gallup supported the idea of a program providing the elderly with medical insurance financed via an increase in Social Security taxes, as opposed to an alternative whereby individuals simply purchased health care policies in the private market. A few months later, in May 1962, support for a public program guaranteeing the elderly access to medical insurance had slipped below 50%. By 1965, just 46% of those surveyed by Gallup wanted the public program as compared to the private alternative.

This decline in support was not due to a lack of interest in the issue. The percentage of Americans in these surveys responding that they had "no opinion" on the matter of government's role in health care stayed constant at about 20%. The shift in opinion represents a popular decline in support for a government guarantee of access to health care. The opposition of powerful interest groups, ranging from the American Medical Association to the National Association of Manufacturers, helped to frame the debate as a choice

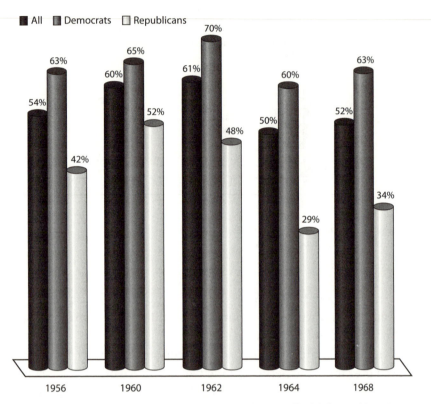

Figure 2.2. Support for Government's Role in Health Care Affordability, 1956–1968
Note: Respondents were asked whether they agreed or disagreed with the statement: "Government out to help people get doctors and hospital care at low cost."
Source: National Election Studies

between socialized medicine—which would require "high taxes, loss of freedom and bureaucratic problems"—and the American way of health care.[6] Decades later, the Clinton administration ran into the same brick wall of opponents and the same framing as they tried to create a more universal health care entitlement. Their effort went nowhere.

Johnson, by contrast, pushed forward with the most significant expansion of federal responsibility for health care in our history, not to mention landmark programs like Head Start, and Nixon proposed an income support plan that was far more progressive than anything

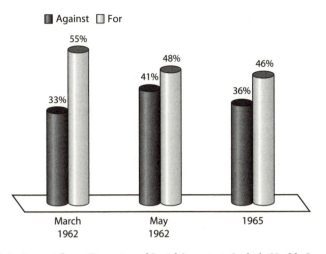

Figure 2.3. Support for an Expansion of Social Security to Include Health Care for the Elderly, 1962–1965
Note: Respondents were asked whether they preferred providing health insurance for the elderly by allowing them to buy private plans or whether government should finance a program through Social Security.
Source: National Election Studies

seen before (and in many ways since). Both presidents moved ahead of public attitudes that were not as expansive as the progressive assumptions underlying their signature policies. The policies rarely survived intact (and in the case of the FAP, failed to pass Congress at all),[7] but both presidents soldiered on and left a legacy behind that we rely on to this day.

THE GREAT SOCIETY: OPPORTUNITY, NOT SECURITY

Though it was not really acceptable to talk about poverty through the 1950s, an increasing awareness of the persistence of poverty amidst plenty—notably in the writings of Galbraith, McCarthy, and especially Harrington—prompted the Kennedy and Johnson administrations to propose an array of antipoverty programs.[8]

Johnson introduced his landmark initiative in May 1964, at a University of Michigan commencement address. Still reeling from the loss of President Kennedy, both Johnson and the audience before him were in need of inspiration, a signature initiative that would help to turn the page. Only two years earlier, Martin Luther King Jr.'s March on Washington had underlined the inextricable link between racial injustice and economic inequality. The urban riots that rocked the country's sense of complacency had not yet erupted.[9] Johnson implored the graduating seniors to join in a noble quest to transform the trajectory of Americans at the bottom of the economic pyramid. "For better or worse," he noted, "your generation has been appointed by history to deal with those problems and to lead America toward a new age."

> You have the chance never before afforded to any people in any age. . . . So will you join in the battle to give every citizen the full equality which God enjoins and the law requires whatever his belief, or race, or the color of his skin? Will you join in the battle to give every citizen an escape from the crushing weight of poverty?
> . . . There are those timid souls who say this battle cannot be won; that we are condemned to a soulless wealth. I do not agree. We have the power to shape the civilizations that we want. But I will need your will, your labor, your hearts, if we are to build that kind of society.[10]

Johnson's acceptance speech at the Democratic convention in 1965 reinforced the same message: in a time of unprecedented affluence, no American should be poor:

> We are in the midst of the largest and longest period of peacetime prosperity in our history. . . . But prosperity for most has not brought prosperity to all. And those who have received the bounty of this land . . . must not now turn from the needs of their neighbors.[11]

While the new Medicare and Medicaid programs were redistributive (and generous, by American standards), they fell far short of the universal health care systems, generous family allowances, universal and free higher education, and highly redistributive tax codes of the

European social democracies. Most of the programs that constituted the War on Poverty emphasized instead state investment in human capital, coupled with a legal assault on discriminatory practices. This outcome was a consequence of a battle between two opposing perspectives, outlined cogently by political scientist Judith Russell.[12] Fiscal Keynesians, led by Walter Heller, believed that appropriate economic policy would stimulate growth and that this, combined with appropriate human capital investment and anti-discrimination enforcement, would permit the persistently poor (who were disproportionately black) to claim their fair share. Structuralists, like Willard Wirtz in the Labor Department, disagreed and advocated a more interventionist policy of job creation. The latter lost and the former won. Hence, what we owe one another—Johnson explained in this speech and elsewhere—is not equality of outcomes or economic security through federal job programs or free health care for all but rather the *chance* to reach one's full potential.

Johnson formally introduced the War on Poverty to Congress in his 1964 State of the Union address with a set of arguments intended to make it clear that this effort would count as a success when every American had the tools, not necessarily the goods.[13] "This budget and this year's legislative program," the president explained, "are designed to help each and every American citizen fulfill his basic hopes." And what were those hopes?

> . . . a fair chance to make good; his hopes for fair play from the law; his hope for a full-time job on full-time pay; his hope for a decent home for his family in a decent community; his hopes for a good school for his children with good teachers; his hopes for security when faced with sickness or unemployment or old age.
>
> Our task is to help replace . . . despair with opportunity. This administration, here and now, declares unconditional war on poverty. . . . It will not be a short or easy struggle, no single weapon or strategy will suffice, but we shall not rest until that war is won. The richest Nation on earth can afford to win it. We cannot afford to lose it.[14]

Johnson's emphasis on capabilities was critical to his argument for the Civil Right Acts of 1964. [15] In a televised address in entitled "America's Promise," Johnson argued that civil rights alone were not enough:

> All Americans must have the privileges of citizenship regardless of race. . . . But I would like to caution you and remind you that to exercise these privileges takes much more than just a legal right. It requires a trained mind and a healthy body . . . people cannot contribute to the Nation if they are never taught to read or write, if their bodies are stunted from hunger, if their sickness goes untended, if their life is spent in hopeless poverty just drawing a welfare check. So we want to open the gates to opportunity. But we are also going to give all our people, black and white, the help that they need to walk through those gates.[16]

The War on Poverty had broad appeal within the Democratic majority coalition because it typified liberal thinking at the time about economic growth and wealth distribution. As communications historian David Zarefsky explains, the War on Poverty was in many ways the apex of the liberal reform efforts of the 1960s:

> [The War on Poverty clearly embodied] the assumptions of the liberal argument: society was benign; "fine tuning" could provide opportunities for those left out, without seriously threatening the interests of the well-to-do; opportunities would translate into results; the values of the middle class were shared by the poor; an expanding economy made it possible to alleviate poverty without redistribution of income or wealth; and the federal government was a fit instrument for carrying out those purposes.[17]

With a focus on "educational opportunity and work preparation," historian Michael Katz argues, the antipoverty agenda "assumed the continuation of growth and abundance . . . [and] depended on the continued expansion and easy availability of jobs." The emphasis on creating opportunity for the poor was inherently conservative insofar as it promised "to solve every social problem without recourse to conflict or redistribution," and in so doing "divert[ed] attention away from the structural barriers to opportunity."[18]

The tepid public response to the redistributive parts of Johnson's program, captured in the opinion polls described earlier in this chapter, stand in contrast to the somewhat more enthusiastic embrace of the human capital agenda. Highly motivated supporters wrote to the White House in the weeks and months that followed his State of the Union address. "I wish particularly to commend your War on Poverty," wrote George Axtelle from Carbondale, Illinois.

> "Absurdity" has become a well worn word—too well worn. But if it were ever appropriate it is when one considers our enormous productivity and our disinherited. . . . Victory in this war will be an achievement without rival—"The poor you will always have with you." What an historic achievement to blot out this terrible fact.[19] (May 5, 1964)

> *New York Herald Tribune* Radio Station WVIP, Mount Kisco, Westchester County, New York, congratulates you on launching the President's War on Poverty. . . . The overwhelming majority of WVIP listeners have responded with complete approval of your program in this vital area. Somewhat to our own surprise, we have found that poverty exists not only in the depressed areas of Appalachia, but also rears its ugly head in the areas of affluent Westchester.[20] (Jean Ensign, President and General Manager WVIP Radio, to Johnson, Mount Kisco, N.Y., Apr. 20, 1964)

> I have been watching with keen interest the progress of your campaign to wipe out poverty in the United States and wish to commend you for it, as I am sure does every loyal American. We recognize that it is a long and slow process as it has taken thirty years since President Roosevelt declared that one-third of the nation was suffering and now it has been reduced to one-fifth.[21] (George Freedley to Johnson, New York City, June 24, 1964)

These supporters were ordinary Americans. But like FDR before him, President Johnson received many letters from people who had professional reasons for their support. Social workers, small-town mayors, and teachers with poorly clothed children in their class-rooms let LBJ know that he was on the right track, and it was about time. Johnson himself had been a teacher of poor Hispanic children in Texas and knew all too well how poverty could derail educational prospects.[22] He heard from many people who had a similar vantage point. Father John Wagner, executive secretary of the Bishops' Com-mittee for the Spanish Speaking in San Antonio, Texas, was witness to the desperation of migrant populations settling along the border. "I have read and reread your State of the Union message," Father Wagner noted, "and I find it a most challenging and orientated [sic] toward a great future."

It is indeed an indictment against all of us that in the past we have permitted such a depression to exist in our affluent society with such resigned complacency. No disadvantaged group in the U.S. will benefit proportionately as much from this all-out war on pov-erty as the Spanish-speaking citizen.[23] (Jan. 10, 1964)

In The War Against Poverty the Counties of Huerfano, Las Animas and Costilla in Colorado have been isolated. These counties, as Senator [John] Carroll once said "never emerged from the great depression." We need help desperately if as Americans we are to contribute to Our Country, and not always Ask From Our Coun-try.[24] (Ernest Sandoval to Johnson, Walsenburg, Colo., July 21, 1964)

The place to begin the whole program is here in South Texas, if there were ever a need for retraining and a new chance for life in a free country this is true in South Texas. The Latin Americans in our region have been exploited until they have no opportunity of equal growth. . . . The retraining of the unemployed and unedu-cated will do more to rebuild our future economy of the individual family unit than anything introduced in our federal system of government since World War II. This is one program that even the most conservative minds cannot honestly object to — even the best-paid Republicans should want to see another human being receive the opportunity to feed himself and become a full-time citizen free of the need for welfare aid.[25] (Bill Lea to Johnson, Alice, Tex., Mar. 18, 1964)

William Hurst, mayor of Irwin, Pennsylvania, had a "day job" as an investigator for the Treasury Department of his state that "[took him] into the homes and other places where poverty and most depressing and frightening living conditions [were] very evident":

> This is truly a disgrace to our great Nation. You are to be most highly commended for the interest you have shown in people living under such terrible conditions. . . . I would like to suggest to you, Sir, that exceptional effort be put forth for the youth of the Land, looking towards jobs and better all around conditions are opportunities. . . .They [youths] are discontented, disillusioned, and in many cases quite bitter.[26] (Apr. 16, 1964)

His observations were seconded by Kenneth West, a commissioner in the Department of Public Welfare in Elmira, New York. "If we are ever going to break the cycle of generation after generation of poverty-stricken oppressed individuals," West told the president, "we must look at the total picture."

> [We must] devise some way to lift the uneducables and the untrainables, too, and their families from the dregs of poverty and despair. It is in these areas that government . . . must play a major role in getting these groups employed with employment that carries the benefits of private employment and is not labeled a relief program.[27] (May 8, 1964)

Muckrakers like Michael Harrington had drawn attention to the Appalachian region, and Martin Luther King had marched thousands to Washington to turn a spotlight on the distress of the big cities, but many other parts of the nation went unrecognized, though they were just as needy. African Americans in small towns, especially in the South, suffered under the dual burden of extreme poverty and a local power structure that shut the door in the face of black leaders. Jerome Holland, who in 1964 was president of the Hampton Institute, a historically black college in Virginia, wrote to Johnson to "applaud the administration's resolve to mobilize the substantial resources of this great country to fight against a pernicious enemy — poverty." But he urged Johnson not to stop there.

> There is one aspect to the war on poverty which is not <u>specifically</u> covered. . . . The war on poverty should also be a war against segregation and discrimination. Most of the poverty abroad in the land today was spawned by these evils. We must be ever alert lest we unwittingly reproduce under new labels those forces which we are seeking to destroy. . . . Therefore, although I support the Economic Opportunity Act of 1964 in principle, I am urging that federal funds not be made available to support undemocratic practices [emphasis in original].

Robert Spike, executive director of the Commission on Religion and Race for the National Council of Churches of Christ, contacted Johnson's trusted adviser, Bill Moyers, to make sure he understood that without a greater emphasis on civil rights, there would be no end to poverty.[28] "We have been very excited here at the Commission by the emphasis in the President's message on an all-out attack on places of poverty in this country," Spike explained.

> This coincides so exactly with a project which is central in our work at the moment, namely, an extensive program in community organization, literacy training and economic redevelopment in the Mississippi Delta. Our extensive involvement in civil rights activities have led us to the conviction that in certain key areas, the civil rights issue is irrevocably tied up with basic human needs for both Negroes and whites.

Young people were considered a particularly urgent target for the War on Poverty. They seemed to be drifting, even in a period of peace and prosperity. Citizens asked Johnson to find a way to use the War on Poverty to pull young people back to the straight and narrow.

> I am very pleased with your "War on Poverty" program, but especially your Job Corps for our youth. Our growing number of young people, who cannot find jobs, are deserving of your program. Perhaps we have gone a bit overboard on science and have neglected vocational training.[29] (George Kramer, mayor of Waukee, Iowa, to Johnson, Mar. 27, 1964)

> The spring thaws and ensuing floods that are upon us serve to remind us that there have been no large scale flood control programs since FDR and the days of Grand Coulee Dam etc. Couldn't this program be reactivated under President Johnson's War on Poverty program so as to serve two useful social purposes? Couldn't the old CCC [Civilian Conservation Corps] idea be used to retrain and train the young people who have not been adequately trained in the conventional educational processes?[30] (Lou Gross to Walter Jenkins, New York City, Mar. 10, 1964)

Of particular concern were young men in the prison system, a population we recognize now as especially likely to spend their lives in poverty. They were comparatively few in number in the 1960s, relative to what we see in the nation's prisons today, but those who worked in the criminal justice system alerted Johnson to the importance of saving these young people before it was too late. Coke Lambert, chaplain of the Harris County Jail in Houston, Texas, reminded the president that "approximately three million persons pass through our County Jails and City Lock-Ups each year."

> May I respectfully suggest that here would be an excellent place to initiate some action in your 'War on Poverty' with people who should be receptive to some realistic program of rehabilitation. . . .

[T]he jail is an excellent place to begin to helping many people to learn to help themselves and learn to live as good citizens.[31] (July 25, 1964)

This morning I read the text of your Tuesday Message to Congress regarding a war on poverty. I was particularly interested in your recommendation that Congress create a Job Corps. . . . I would suggest that the "National Work-Training Program" include some type of disciplinary training. While I am not advocating strict military regimentation, our experience in the Department of Corrections—where forty per cent of our 12,000 inmates are under the age of twenty-four—indicates that most of these young people have never experienced any discipline, either externally or internally imposed.[32] (George Beto, director, Texas Board of Corrections, to Johnson, Huntsville, Tex., Mar. 17, 1964)

Opposition to the Great Society

The Johnson archives are full of letters that endorse the president's ambition to rid a prosperous nation of the scourge of poverty. They come from every corner of the country, from obscure rural towns and big cities, from the heart of the Deep South to the big cities of the Rust Belt. But public opinion polls tell us that the sentiments of the public at large were far more mixed, and the archives reflect this oppositional trail as well.

Americans had clear favorites among the Great Society programs, and the War on Poverty was not one of them. The public was mildly supportive of federal provision of medical care for the aged and funding for education programs, but these aspects of Johnson's plans were far more popular than his "antipoverty" programs, which trailed in at only 8%. Indeed, even in the contentious mid-1960s, voting rights for Negroes enjoyed more public support than antipoverty programs.

Public sympathy for the poor did not increase with time. As the War on Poverty marched on, ever larger segments of the public viewed poverty as a result of lack of effort on the part of the poor rather than as the consequence of circumstances beyond an individual's control.

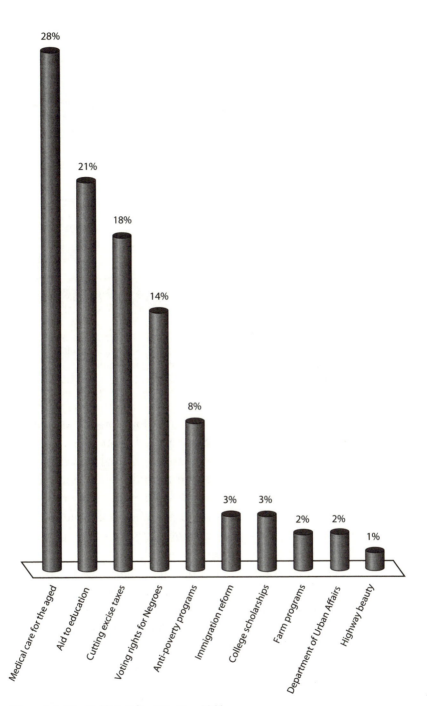

Figure 2.4. The Public's Policy Priorities, 1965
Note: Categories reflect the original Harris poll phrasing.
Source: Louis Harris & Associates, December 1965

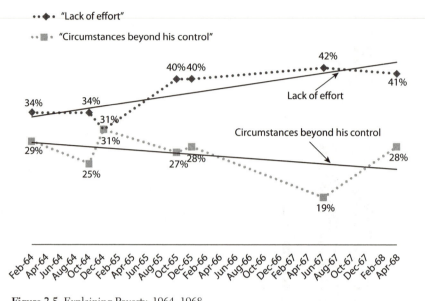

Figure 2.5. Explaining Poverty, 1964–1968
Note: Respondents were asked to respond to the question: "Which is more often to blame if a person is poor: lack of effort, or circumstances beyond his control?"
Source: Gallup and the National Opinion Research Center Surveys, 1965–1968

In November 1964, just eleven months after Johnson introduced the Great Society to the nation in his State of the Union address, public opinion on the cause of poverty was evenly divided between "lack of effort" and "circumstances" beyond an individual's control. Yet in the years to follow, increasing numbers blamed the poor for their poverty. By April 1968, 41% blamed poverty on a lack of effort by the poor, compared to just 28% who saw poverty as the consequences of circumstances beyond an individual's control.

The skeptics were not shy about expressing their views to LBJ, and the Johnson archives contain just as many letters from detractors trying to set the president straight as they do supportive commentaries. Many of his correspondents were convinced that the poor simply could not be helped out of their condition, at least not to the point of self-sufficiency. As one Ohio resident put the matter, the president's plan was laudable but based on a fundamental misunderstanding of what made people poor in the first place. "You must surely know that you cannot eradicate poverty any more than you can eradicate personalities in people," Robert Culbertson explained from Akron. Ethel Brosius wrote in from Houston to Jack Valenti, a special aid to President Johnson, agreeing with the thrust of Culbertson's comments.[33] "With the money the President is planning to spend on this particular war," she complains, "why not a war to revive some our earliest virtues?"

> Honesty, integrity, thrift, GUTS, independence, desire for and appreciation of freedom, perseverance, "stick-to-itiveness," efficiency, respect for property, and understanding of moral responsibility, education, etc. . . . This kind of war would be a positive rather than a negative approach to the problem, and would certainly be less expensive and much more constructive in the long run.[34] (Ethel Brosius to Jack Valenti, Houston, Tex., no date; probably early May 1964; emphasis in original)

> I have read with interest of the <u>anti-poverty program</u> now underway. I agree with its objectives; however, if the program is to be a stopgap, palliative, giveaway program it will fail because it will merely substitute poverty of the spirit for poverty of the wallet. . . . Our American creed puts financial independence first: the one who fails is looked upon as less a man than he should have been. Thus, going on the dole takes away one's manhood, a traumatic experience to a self-respecting man the first time it happens.[35] (Harold Van Coops to Johnson, Albany, Calif., no date, last quarter 1964; emphasis in original)

By 1965, criticism of the War on Poverty reached a crescendo on the left and the right. Corruption or mismanagement of one kind or another was an increasingly common concern. A Gallup poll from 1965 reported that 48% of respondents believed corruption and political favoritism in Washington were increasing over time, and 40% felt corruption was increasing among state officials.[36] Fifty-six percent believed that "there has been too much politics in the antipoverty program."[37] Complaints about the misallocation of antipoverty funds; inadequate resources; monies denied or withheld from specific regions, community members, or their organized representatives by local and state governments; extravagant costs; and even outright graft flooded the White House mailroom:

> By the time the political favorites, and the crooked politicians get through with the appropriation for fighting poverty there will be none left for the poor, for whom it was supposed to be. Does the President know about these grafty salaries? Who has the authority to appoint these crooks and name their salaries?[38] (Mr. and Mrs. R. Carroll to George Reedy, El Paso, Tex., May 20, 1965)

> We, the members of <u>the underground</u>, demand that you recommit yourself to the War on Poverty and the Community Action Program, in particular. In your State of the Union Message tonight, we want you to ask for 1) supplemental appropriations to fully carry out the War on Poverty this year 2) increased appropriations for the War on Poverty in Fiscal Year, 1968. The War on Poverty <u>must</u> be escalated! We, the poor in the world's richest nation, cannot continue to believe in great national ventures such as an Asian war or trips to the moon, when we see the low wages we get, the poor education provided our children in public schools, and the crummy, high-rent housing we live in. You must help us change this by supporting a vital Community Action Program.[39] (Unsigned "open letter" to Johnson, hand-delivered to the White House Mail Room by a member of a group picketing outside, Jan. 10, 1967; emphasis in original)

Maximum Feasible Obstruction

The organizational structure of the War on Poverty served several purposes at the same time. It streamed funds into job training, early childhood education, and community health care by supporting the burgeoning ranks of nonprofit organizations. By directing funds to the grass roots, though, Johnson was looking to achieve a second goal: to cultivate the leadership of minority communities around the country for the Democratic Party, bypassing the urban machines and traditional power structures that had long had a lock on patronage. "Maximum feasible participation," the slogan that was supposed to describe the modus operandi of the Office of Economic Opportunity, spoke directly to the aspirations of African American leaders who wanted to define the direction of antipoverty programs for themselves.

It did not take long for citizens and leaders to let the president know that his plans were being thwarted at every turn. Minority leaders found themselves outmaneuvered by local sheriffs, the white mayors of black towns, and well-known racists, who were not about to let African Americans take control. Complaints poured in, particularly from the Jim Crow South. Baxton Bryant, executive director of the Tennessee Council on Human Rights in Nashville, expressed "great concern about the future of the Office of Economic Opportunity [especially] . . . the Community Action Program":

> With all due respect to our southern federal officials, many of them are not showing much enthusiasm for real acceptance of the Negro race as fellow human beings. We believe that your eloquent address at Howard University in which you advocated not only granting equal treatment at present but restitution for past deeds is the blue print for a new America.[40] (Aug. 24, 1966)

Bryant's concerns were shared by liberal activists all over the South. Congressmen wrote to him to alert him to the way the program was being derailed by the power grabs under way in communities where African Americans could do little to stop it. "[We] urge immediate investigation of [the] appointment of Indianola, Mississippi police chief Bryce Alexander to head Sunflower County . . . poverty program," telegraphed Congressmen Augustus Hawkins and Joseph Resnick. "Alexander's record of racist terror against Negroes makes his appointment absolutely monstrous and unthinkable."[41]

Roger Bell, a black leader who had been authorized to "take the lead and organize a country wide program," wrote to Lady Bird Johnson from Guadalupe, Texas, to protest his removal from the local economic opportunity office:

> We are afraid the program is being abused in this, and we as Negroes, have been denied to whole key Officers and our voting in the Organizing of the War on Poverty Program. . . . When the Whites

in High places and Elbert Jandt, Lawyer, saw it was going over and
money in the program to help the lower level peoples they took
over and kick me out.[42] (Seguin, Tex., June 8, 1965)

Sargent Shriver was bombarded by similar complaints from African American leaders in Alabama. "We indignantly protest and refuse to be humiliated by being subjected to the acceptance of a
community action committee which by its very composition and the
manner in which it was formed clearly controverts the philosophy of
the Economic Opportunity Act and the war against poverty."

Sir, the basic philosophy of the war against poverty is that communities by organizing among themselves can obtain the means to help
themselves to eliminate the causes and conditions of poverty. The
Sumter County Movement for Human Rights . . . [has] sought to
organize and proceed to bring social and economic change to the
majority of our county's population. . . . The cause of much of the
Negro community's poverty has been the pressure and imprint of
racial segregation and exploitation. [Alabama OEO Director] Mr.
[Claude] Kirk's creation, the Area 14 Community Action Committee, only can maintain the racial discrimination and exploitation of
the past.[43] (Sumter County Movement for Human Rights, c/o Reverend R. H. Upton, to Sargent Shriver, York, Ala., Aug. 8, 1965)

African Americans were not alone in their fury. Latinos in the
border states also found themselves excluded from leadership roles
and feared the diversion of funds intended for their communities
into the hands of Anglos, who would send the money to their own.
Daniel Castro, a leader in the San Diego area, wrote to Rudy Ramos,
the director of the Washington, D.C., office of the American GI Forum, hoping to enlist his help in presenting his protest to the White
House:

It has been our experience here in San Diego that the Mexican-
American is not even remotely considered for responsible positions
of employment in the "war on poverty" agencies. The average "An-

glo" agency Chief or Director, as the case may be, is traditionally incapable of thinking of the Mexican-American as top echelon material even though we have fully qualified, competent and capable people to fill these positions. And to add insult to injury, these "Anglo" heads of departments could not care less about our problems. We are not going to plead any special compensatory consideration of our case as the Negro has done. But we are going to demand equal opportunity.[44] (May 20, 1965)

Native Americans in the Midwest also faced obstacles in claiming their rightful place as heads of local economic opportunity agencies:

I am calling your attention to a most serious situation existing in Comanche County Oklahoma. . . . Senator Fred R Harris is involved in perpetuating these racist activities by his influence apparently being used to see that all white people are hired in top positions in the poverty program here in Comanche County and in Cotton County Oklahoma.[45] (Lonnie Johnson to Johnson, Lawton, Okla., Jan. 11, 1968)

While the Deep South and the border regions of the Southwest were particularly problematic places for the federal government to reach down and overturn local power structures, the problem was not confined to those areas. Californians and New Yorkers also felt the brunt of racial exclusion.

We have existed with volunteer leadership from the Negro community since June of 1965, while the funding for the project has been postponed over and over. During this period numerous projects have been funded without delay for a number of public and private agencies for several hundred thousand dollars in other cities. . . . We believe it to be significant that the only program prepared, led and supported by Negro low income leadership in Contra Costa county should also be the only program delayed for nearly a year and also the only program subject to political conditions.[46] (N. Eldridge to Johnson, Mar. 16, 1966)

We did not anticipate the pitfalls that are being set before us by those vested with power and find it so easy to usurp for reasons most obvious, but questionable. . . . We have mobilized and utilized all community resources! We have developed, conducted and administered with maximum feasible participation the poor themselves! We have set forth the machinery for motion, for action, and they tells us our efforts, our work, our needs are not valid! What authoritarian right has the Office of Economic Opportunity to question the poor and their eventual uplift? What right does this office have to determine the destinies of the residents involved in a poverty culture? . . . How can they sit there in their tribunal atmosphere and decide that the poor need not legal opportunity services; that they need not jobs, etc., when they are knowledgeable in this county's failure to provide clinical services for the poor and medically indigent. . . . This is no logic! It is a method of madness whereby the people are again 'stripped' of hope, of respect, of confidence in those who constantly assume the right to determine their destinies. . . . Perhaps, we will never dream; perhaps the War on Poverty is nothing more than a Shakespearean farce that plays through the Mid-Summer on into all seasons.[47] (William Larregui to Johnson, Apr. 14, 1966)

Race and ethnic divisions were the dominant fault line, but there were others as well. Small communities and towns were often muscled out by larger, more politically connected cities in the race to capture the federal funding for local nonprofits.

I am now led to believe that the Office of Economic Opportunity or at least its San Francisco regional office, is arbitrarily making decisions to completely discriminate against small counties. . . . We have a large proportion of American Indians and other deprived people in our community who would very much benefit from the provision of the Economic Opportunity Act, but we find that we are told, in effect, that if we want to take advantage of the provisions of this act, we have to move our poor people to the city. I hope that this disgusting and disgraceful example against America's newest

minority—the rural people of America, who have neither influence or votes, may receive the consideration it deserves.[48] (Paul
Kreuzenstein to Johnson, Alturas, Calif., May 13, 1966)

Critics on the left took Johnson to task for not putting enough muscle
behind what they saw as a fundamentally good idea. They blamed
him for weak implementation that enabled local power structures to
move in on the funds intended for community empowerment. Eventually, their frustrations exploded into the welfare rights movement,
which demanded a place for recipients, especially African American
and Latina women, at the federal and state tables where welfare benefits were set.[49]

Conservatives, on the other hand, were incensed because they
thought LBJ's vision of maximum feasible participation was well on
its way to being realized, with authority and money flowing to the
worst left-wing elements, the black nationalists. Only three months
after Johnson's speech at the University of Michigan, Harlem went
up in flames. Not long thereafter, Watts, Newark, and dozens of
other major and minor cities were convulsed by riots. Between 1965
and 1968 more than three hundred riots occurred, resulting in two
hundred deaths and the destruction of several thousand businesses.[50]
The taxpaying Right was in no mood to see its hard-earned cash go
to people who were breaking shop windows, pointing guns at the
police, and screaming "burn, baby, burn" at small business owners
located in the ghettos.

The reality was a good deal more complicated. Black activists were
aware that their own communities had the most to lose from urban
unrest and were among the most zealous peacemakers, trying to put
a stop to the mayhem. Others were sympathetic to the frustration,
if not the methods, of rioters, seeing in these urban explosions the
unavoidable consequences of years of discrimination and economic
disenfranchisement. Many believed that lack of opportunity for employment was at the heart of the racial unrest. Indeed, a nationally-
representative poll by Louis Harris in the fall of 1967 reports that
a substantial majority believed federal investment in employment
programs would help stem racial unrest, a path Johnson eschewed.

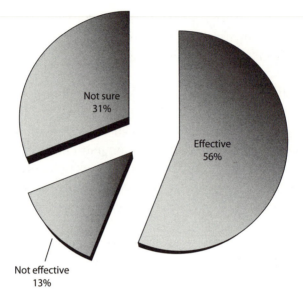

Figure 2.6. Public Works as an Effective Solution to America's Racial Unrest, 1967
Note: Respondents were asked to respond to the question: "Would a large-scale federal work project to give jobs to America's unemployed be an effective way to resolve the race problem in America?"
Source: Louis Harris & Associates 1967 survey, as reported in the *Washington Post*

More than any other incident, the grant provided by the Office of Economic Opportunity to Harlem's Black Arts Repertory Theater in 1965 set the stage for a public rebuke of the whole War on Poverty by conservative citizens. Founded by poet and playwright LeRoi Jones (later Amiri Baraka), the theater received a federal grant that was used to support theater pieces endorsing racial separatism, encouraging militancy, and calling openly for violent rebellion. When the grant was publicized, public reaction was instantaneous and incandescent. How could Johnson have spent hard-earned tax dollars on this kind of trash, angry citizens wanted to know.

I cannot express in strong enough terms how much I protest my tax money being spent to produce plays of hate. . . . I would like your personal assurance that all Federal money will be withdrawn [from the Black Arts Repertory Theater] and all possible effort will be made to see that such a thing does not happen in the future.[51] (Walter [illegible] to Johnson, Beverly Hills, Calif., Dec. 1, 1965)

What gives? Our government has been foolish in its expenditure of funds in many instances, but never have I heard of such a horrible example as [the Black Arts Repertory Theater]. . . . Are you in Washington so naïve as to believe that you are an independent entity and can hand out doles to suit your own interests? . . . A portion of the income tax we pay is taken from my husband's Navy retirement. Does it make sense that some of this money should go to a vile man who not only wants to overthrow our government, but as a result of this fiasco, will be teaching impressionable young people the art of anarchy?[52] (Jean Gettle to Johnson, Tillamook, Ore., December 1965)

If the misuse of tax dollars was the major frustration, a second and equally powerful objection had to do with encouraging antiwhite sentiments among black people. Critics wondered how a program premised on the need to eradicate racism could justify supporting an arts program dedicated to raising racial tension and hatred of whites. Since the story broke in the aftermath of some of the nation's worst race riots, at a time when photographs of injured police were splashed across the front pages of the newspapers, it took little imagination to link Jones's plays to the urban nightmare. "I am so disturbed that our money, namely, $40,000.00 in federal antipoverty funds is enabling LeRoi Jones to foster hate, brutality, and segregation against the very white people who are trying to help the Negroes," wrote Mrs. R. B. King from Plainfield, New Jersey.

Kindly answer me as to why our funds are going to this venomous type of organization with a mentally twisted leader who is trying to tear down our glorious America and not to people who could be educated to be decent American citizens.[53] (Dec. 2, 1965)

Americans had always expressed only tepid support, at best, for Johnson's Great Society ambitions. The response to the urban unrest of the 1960s exposed the cracks in the foundation of broad public support for the Great Society policies and set up the state for decades of tension around political elites' efforts to expand the welfare state.

By 1966, Vietnam was bleeding the national coffers dry; the Great Society was forced to retrench. "Because of Vietnam," Johnson acknowledged, "we cannot do all that we should, or all that we would like to do."[54] Indeed, 46% of the American public agreed, and believed that federal government should redirect funding from the War on Poverty toward the conflict in Vietnam.[55] Johnson's final State of the Union address, in January 1969, acknowledged that much was left undone, but urged the country to hold fast to "commitments that all of us have made together that will, if we carry them out, give America our best chance to achieve the kind of great society that we all want."[56] Included in the targets left unmet were an urban development bank to fund the growing need for investment in the inner cities, funding for urban home construction, "more adequate" child and maternal health care, an increase in social security benefits, catastrophic medical insurance, and funds for job training.

Johnson listed his successes: Medicare, voting rights, federal aid to schools, Head Start, environmental protection, federal job training programs, and the lowest unemployment rate (and the highest rate of job growth) in over a decade. They constitute the remarkable legislative record on which we trade to this day. But they were achieved in the face of declining public support for his progressive spirit. What began as modest support for the redistributive aspects of the Great Society fell off sharply over time. The most durable public commitment was to the human capital agenda, which aimed to provide the least fortunate with more tools to compete for educational and occupational opportunity.

Nixon's Liberal Legacy

In 1969, the year Nixon arrived in the White House, the nation's welfare system was surrounded by a near-complete collapse of public confidence. The War on Poverty had bolstered participation in the Aid to Families with Dependent Children (AFDC) program, with greater public attention to the program and outreach to eligible families bringing a steady stream of needy Americans onto the rolls (table 2.1). The general public reacted with a combustible combination of frustration and concern. Seventy-four percent of respondents to a Gallup poll conducted in 1969 believed that at least half of those receiving welfare could "earn their own way if they really wanted to," while 84% of the respondents to the National Opinion Research Center survey taken that year agreed with the view that "there are too many people receiving welfare money who should be working." By 1971, 89% believed the welfare rolls were full of those who should be working.

The hostility toward welfare recipients, and the sense that government had bent over backward for the wrong constituency was unmistakable. Sixty-two percent believed that the rolls were bloated with welfare cheats who "actually earn more on the side without reporting it." Eighty-six percent of respondents to a Yankelovich, Skelly and White survey agreed with the statement, "There is more concern today for the welfare bum who doesn't want to work than for the hard working person who is struggling to make a living." And 73% endorsed the idea that communities that provided food and clothing to individuals on relief should reduce their cash grants to reflect that contribution. Martin Gilen's important book, *Why Americans Hate Welfare*, shows convincingly that the public's impatience lay not with the welfare state in general but rather with one program alone: public

Table 2.1 Public Mistrust of Welfare Recipients during the Nixon Years

At least half of the people on welfare could earn their own way if they really wanted to (1969)	74%
There are too many people on welfare who should be working (1969)	84%
There are too many people on welfare who should be working (1971)	89%
Many people getting welfare payments actually earn more on the side without reporting it (1971)	62%
There is more concern today for the welfare bum than for the hard-working person who is struggling to make a living (1974)	86%

Sources: Gallup, 1969; National Opinion Research Corporation, 1969 and 1971; Yankelovitch, Skelly, and White, 1974.

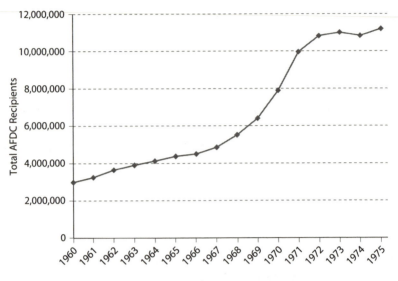

Figure 2.7. AFDC Participation, 1960–1975
Sources: Department of Health and Human Services, "Annual Report to Congress: In-
dicators of Welfare Dependence" (2002); Department of Health and Human Services
Administration for Children and Families, "AFDC/TANF Caseload Data, 1960–1999"

assistance to the able-bodied, which was popularly understood to be
a "black" program.[57]

Even so, Americans seemed unwilling to dismantle a system they
thoroughly disliked. Most (77%) thought it important that "adequate
living standards for the needy" be provided through welfare programs
and by a large measure *disagreed* with the claim that "money spent
on welfare is just wasted and doesn't really help anyone."[58] Progressive views were riddled with reactionary holes since, by a large margin, Americans thought that welfare made people lazy or that only
lazy people were on welfare.

While the explicit racial attitudes would appear to account for
the harsh anti-welfare attitudes of the 1960s, 1970s, and most of all
the 1980s, the view that relief recipients were morally compromised
long predated this period. The association of public assistance with
the undeserving stretches right back to the Depression, when the
public image of relief was at least as much that of the "Okie," the
poor white migrants from the dustbowl, as it was of racial minorities. The harsh reception given to these internal refugees—from the

draconian vagrancy laws to the exploitative labor conditions of the migrant camps—was coupled with antagonism toward virtually any kind of cash relief and only slightly less hostility toward work relief. The targets of that animus were poor whites at least as much as, if not more than, blacks.[59]

Historian William Brock argues that the public expressed "extremely hostile local attitudes" toward the unemployed, particularly transient men in state-run labor camps, during the early Depression.[60] These attitudes were "deeply rooted in tradition," which dictated that "all transients were hobos, scroungers, and would-be criminals," and reflected fears that transients would become at best a burden to local treasuries and at worst a danger to local communities. Historians also emphasize this notion of a qualitative difference between an older pauper class and the new unemployed, who came from a range of social classes and occupational groups. For example, Robert Bremner suggests that "the distinction Roosevelt and the New Deal made between the unemployed and the chronic dependents, and the special status accorded the 'employables,' made for a more favorable public attitude toward, and a better self-image among, the unemployed."[61]

Nonetheless, the association of welfare with African Americans in the Great Society era and the period of Nixon's presidency intensified. As Katz argues, "more than any other single development, in the late 1950s and early 1960s the massive migration of southern blacks to northern cities framed the formulation of both urban and antipoverty policy."[62] The concentration and increasing visibility of poor blacks in the ghettoes of northern cities weakened the association of poverty with rural whites in faraway Appalachia, while the liberalization of eligibility restrictions led to a huge increase in the people receiving direct federal assistance from the AFDC program and a pronounced "changing racial composition" of the welfare rolls throughout the 1960s.

Daniel Moynihan's 1965 Labor Department report, *The Negro Family*, which sought to explain entrenched poverty among black urban communities, changed the way the public thought about poverty. The report itself emphasizes both structural and cultural factors that created powerful disadvantages, but its public reception emphasized the latter to a much greater extent. The "pathology" of the matriarchal family took center stage as the root cause of African American poverty. The image did not endear the burgeoning poor black population of northeastern cities to the white middle and working classes.[63]

At the same time, having won landmark civil rights battles in 1964 and 1965, the civil rights movement turned its attention to expanding economic rights and, combined with incipient black nationalism, shifted the movement's public image from a nonthreatening, supplicant, southern one to a potentially violent, demanding, northern one. This impression was made tangible by the urban riots that burst onto the public consciousness in Watts in 1965 and then came with increasing frequency over the next few years.

Watts was immediately associated with the social pathologies implicated in the Moynihan Report (published just months earlier) by the media and in the public eye.[64] The Los Angeles riots became the first in a chain of events that would push a substantial segment of the American electorate to the right.[65] The combined effect of the Moynihan Report and Watts meant the behavior of the poor—and most particularly of the black poor—rather than any privations or injustices they endured came to the fore in the minds of many Americans when they thought about the issue of poverty.

The news media were largely responsible for the linkage. Overrepresentation of African Americans in stories about public assistance created a tidal wave of race-based animus toward the program. By overwhelming majorities, whites who responded to a 1970 Virginia Slims poll opined that they would be upset if "[their] community decided to increase the amount of money given to blacks on welfare."[66]

The Nixon administration commissioned a set of polls from the National Opinion Research Corporation in 1971 designed to assess public views of welfare and the results indicate the same pronounced distaste for this form of poor relief. Fifty-three percent were in favor of reducing the size of welfare payments and making it harder to qualify in order to avoid raising taxes. Eight-four percent endorsed requiring able-bodied recipients to take "whatever kind of work is available." Nearly the entire universe of respondents (95%) agreed

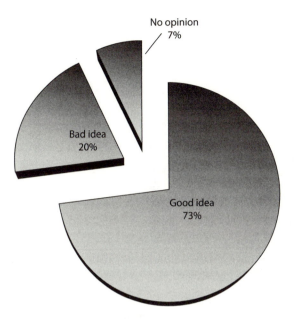

Figure 2.8. Support for Cutting Cash Relief, 1964
Respondents were asked to respond to the question: "What do you think of the idea of decreasing cash relief for those receiving clothes and food?"
Source: Louis Harris & Associates, 1964 survey

that able-bodied welfare recipients should be cut from the rolls if they refused to take a job.

This was the climate within which the Nixon administration tried to push through its own reform agenda. The president turned to his poverty guru, Daniel Patrick Moynihan, to assess the social climate that had increased the "social acceptability of welfare." Nixon wanted to know why the rolls had climbed. Was it that "people [are] more willing to accept welfare than in the past? Has some prior restraint, some feeling of guilt or shame, or whatever, given way to a more permissive [climate]?" Moynihan answered, loudly: "Yes. There seems to have been some change in attitude. Welfare would seem to be less stigmatizing now than in the past."

Moynihan acknowledged that this finding "derived as much from logic as from research." Compared to the 1930s, the country had seen a "general rise in government support payments of various

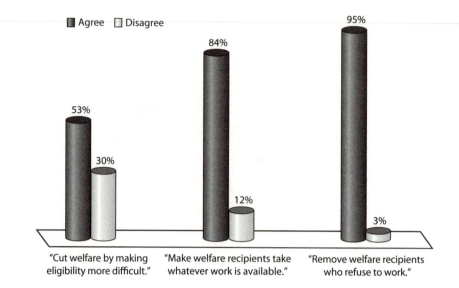

Figure 2.9. Welfare Policy Preferences, 1971
Source: Nixon administration–era poll administered by the National Election Studies, 1971

kinds." He concluded that the "onset of black militancy . . . and the welfare rights movement, and . . . the immense prosperity of the 1960s has made the public more permissive generally." Even so, Moynihan argued, the public remained conflicted, "torn between the tradition of self-reliant individualism and a generous concern for all." And he emphasized that divisions of opinion by race were over-hyped. While "[n]egroes have been more 'permissive' about welfare than whites," Moynihan noted, polling data indicated an "increasing feeling among both negroes and whites that individual lack of initiative is more responsible than outside forces for a person being in poverty" and further that "these general public attitudes are found among the poor also, including those on welfare."[67]

It is ironic, to put it mildly, that the centerpiece of Nixon's domestic policy was not to dismantle welfare but, if anything, to significantly increase its reach to include, for the first time, the nation's working poor. Nixon announced the Family Assistance Plan on August 8, 1969, in a televised address to the nation:

I propose that the federal government build a foundation under the income of every American family with dependent children that cannot care for itself—wherever in America that family may live.

Nixon's plan would have guaranteed a base annual income to all families with dependent children, originally set at $1,600 for a family of four.[68] FAP would replace AFDC, which, Nixon said in his speech, must be "done away with completely," because "It breaks up homes. It often penalizes work. It robs recipients of dignity. And it grows."[69]

FAP effectively functioned as an income supplement. A negative income tax, FAP established a floor on annual earnings at which the tax rate would be zero; a family with no annual earnings would be taxed at a "negative" rate until the earnings reached the zero-rate floor, which would become a minimum guaranteed income. The minimum income would vary by size of family, and the negative rate would be incrementally reduced so as to encourage the poor to work (work would not automatically eliminate benefits; rather, so long as earnings remained below the minimum guaranteed income, earnings would supplement benefits and thus increase a family's annual earnings). As Jill Quadagno writes about the FAP guaranteed income proposal, "As family earnings rose, benefits would be reduced fifty cents for each dollar until they reached zero and the family was supported entirely by earnings. Thus, a family of four with an employed household head would be considerably better off than a welfare family, since benefits combined with earnings could reach $3,810. By contrast, a family of four with no working members, that is, a welfare family, would receive $1,600 a year."[70]

Economist Milton Friedman believed the negative income tax ought to have been provided across the board, available to anyone who fell below a given income threshold regardless of whether or not that person was in the labor force.[71] Such a program was a simple and inexpensive (relative to public employment, for example) way of addressing the market failures and individual human capital deficiencies that led to poverty. Friedman's solution was, however, politically untenable. The welfare system Nixon inherited was premised on the notion that nonworking mothers—rather than intact families, single men, or single working mothers—were the appropriate target of AFDC support. The system Nixon wanted to put in its place was a departure from this model, but it didn't fully embrace Friedman's approach either.

By guaranteeing an annual income to families with dependent children, Nixon was proposing to dramatically increase the welfare rolls by including the working poor, including married couples whose annual earnings were low enough that they fell below the minimum guaranteed income. What the FAP didn't do was address the underlying reasons that poor workers earned so little. Unlike the Great Society approach, the FAP did not provide for better education, health care, housing, or any other form of investment in the well-being of those at the bottom. Nixon's approach did nothing to rearrange the deck of cards that left some groups perpetually on the bottom. It simply raised the standard of living at the bottom by providing more money.

Although the FAP represented a significant enlargement of government contributions to the well-being of the poor, it would not do to emphasize the progressive aspects of the legislation in a climate of public reservations. Moynihan, the primary architect of Nixon's welfare reform agenda, later would reflect that "there was as near as can be to *no* political support for a guaranteed income" (emphasis in original). "Majority opinion [was] clearly disposed to favor plans for dealing with problems of poverty and welfare dependency, *so long as the stigma of 'something for nothing' could be avoided*" (emphasis added).[72]

Accordingly, as noted by sociologist Brian Steensland in his history of guaranteed income policies in the United States, the administration tailored its FAP message to maximize popular support in various and often conflicting camps, most notably and significantly with conservative critics of the existing welfare system.[73] Nixon adviser John Ehrlichman outlined an "Action Plan" that included targeting "key media centers" to brief editorial boards. "The major theme to be used in the briefings has got to be that the present system is terrible."[74]

Nixon staffer Harry Haldeman made a similar point, and underscored the proposal's insistence on work requirements. "Please be sure that all our people who are talking on welfare pick up the President's line and emphasize the point that our purpose is not to get more people on welfare, but to get people off welfare, and to make the point that we do not believe an able-bodied person who refuses to work should be provided with welfare."[75] Speechwriter William Safire recommended that the administration move away from the term "welfare" and rely instead on "workfare" to try to distinguish Nixon's ideas from the status quo, a rhetorical point Nixon embraced. Accordingly, Nixon played up the "conservative rhetoric" when he announced the FAP in a nationally televised speech. Sixty times in the thirty-five-minute speech he spoke the words "work," "jobs," or words rooted in "work," and the administration emphasized that the objective of the plan's work incentives was to get rid of a system that rewarded those who chose *not* to work and encouraged dependency.

Public opinion polls reflect the immense popularity of connecting public assistance with work. Ninety-five percent believed that able-bodied welfare recipients who refused work should be booted from the rolls, while 79% believed that welfare receipt should be connected to mandatory work. The only group about which the public expressed any true ambivalence regarding connecting welfare with work was mothers of school-aged children: only 49% believed mothers should be required to accept a job rather than receive welfare benefits. The prohibition against working motherhood was lifted when children were perceived to be at risk.

As Quadagno notes, the FAP fit into Nixon's and the Republican Party's efforts "to woo an alienated working class by moving racial issues to the periphery" by doing away with the reviled AFDC program altogether and replacing it with a race-blind guaranteed income that also extended aid to the working poor.[76] It would eliminate "equal opportunity from the agenda of the welfare state," and by doing so placate those white voters who resented the association of antipoverty programs with blacks and civil rights. FAP "reward[ed] the deserving working poor" and "resoundingly reaffirmed the Protestant ethic by

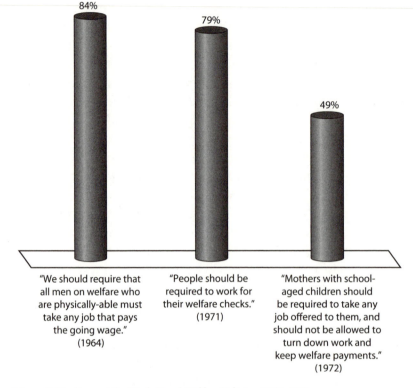

84%

79%

49%

"We should require that
all men on welfare who
are physically-able must
take any job that pays
the going wage."
(1964)

"People should be
required to work for
their welfare checks."
(1971)

"Mothers with school-
aged children should
be required to take any
job offered to them, and
should not be allowed to
turn down work and
keep welfare payments."
(1972)

Figure 2.10. Support for Work-Based Welfare Policies, 1964–1971
Sources: Gallup, 1964; National Opinion Research Corporation, 1971; Gallup, 1972.

promising to force those welfare loafers to get a job. . . . Reducing inequity between the working poor and the welfare poor," Quadagno notes, "became a euphemism for reducing what whites perceived as racial inequity in the tax/benefit ratio."[77]

Though the national economy would continue to grow until the early 1970s, rising inflation and cost of living by the later 1960s were undermining the financial well-being of working people, whose grasp on middle-class stability was already tenuous at best. As the purchasing power of the average blue-collar worker fell steadily, historian Brendan Sexton notes, such workers received none of the sympathy and support of the "welfare-dependent" poor: "Skilled workers are the aristocrats of labor; yet the median earnings of male craftsmen who were employed full-time in 1968 was only $7,978," well below the $9,076 income the Department of Labor set as a "moderate standard of living" for a family of four.[78]

Even amid the affluence of the 1960s there remained "deep economic, social, and geographical segregation between workers and the middle class that approaches the distinction between black and white." Journalist Richard Lemon, analyzing a study Gallup did for *Newsweek* in 1969 in an article titled "The Troubled American," noted that for these "middle Americans, money is something that must be carefully and constantly watched." Ballooning tax rates to cover federal antipoverty programs that seemed to benefit only the minority poor, government-backed efforts to increase black labor market participation, and federally imposed integration chafed at middle Americans, who were protectively "jealous of their union membership," concerned about investments in their homes, and "resistant to Negro demands which seem to threaten that equity."[79]

Under these conditions, a "workfare" framework seemed the best rhetorical bet for the Nixon administration, but its more conservative members were not persuaded. Policy adviser Martin Anderson wrote to Nixon, wary that "Senate leaders continue to oppose FAP in its present form and insist on stronger work requirements." He suggested that Nixon "drop the 'working poor.' . . . While the working poor provision of FAP eats up the bulk of the welfare reform money, the political returns (except from social science academicians) are apt to be small. . . . I doubt that the average American feels strongly about subsidizing the working poor." Doing this might disappoint liberal supporters of the proposal, "but the vast majority of Americans are not even fully aware of the 'working poor' provision of FAP, and, of those who are, I suspect that as many oppose it as support it."[80]

Nixon speechwriter Pat Buchanan echoed the same sentiments in a letter he wrote to Ehrlichman, worrying on paper that Nixon was "liable to go down in history . . . as the President who doubled the welfare rolls; the man who did more than anyone else to destroy the work ethic in America, by bringing the 'working poor' into welfare, men and women who were themselves moving into the lower middle class before being dragged back." Buchanan felt that the "working poor" proposal was the most dangerous and that without it, "we have something that can go through" Congress. "Has any thought been given to . . . providing the incompetent poor with services, i.e. Food Stamps, medical stamps, transportation stamps, etc. instead of with cold cash, which they are unqualified to spend wisely?"[81]

We remember Nixon for his appeal to white, "hard-hat," working-class men and women fed up with the notion that they should bank-roll the nonworking poor and rioting minorities. Yet his administration also tried to court moderate black and civil rights groups while trying to beat back vocal critics on the left, especially activists in the welfare rights movement.[82] Soon after the FAP was proposed, the administration was debating how to respond to "hysterical charges" that welfare rights advocate George Wiley had made against the plan,[83] dispatching the "Family Assistance Working Group . . . through the South knocking these statements down. They have suggested that [civil rights leader] James Farmer also begin speaking on behalf of the welfare program, and he will soon do so."[84]

By mid-January, Moynihan was meeting with "the leadership Conference on Civil Rights to discuss Family Assistance," which "included representatives of fifty or so organizations." He reported back on his success: "It was certainly the friendliest meeting I have had with any such group in the past year. . . . One group after another declared its support for Family Assistance," and the Urban League promised to begin a public relations campaign in support of the plan.[85]

In his history of the FAP, Steensland argues that the African American community offered only lukewarm support for the proposal.[86] Whitney Young, the Urban League leader actively courted by Moynihan, did indeed issue a statement in support of the FAP, but it offered only reserved support, and called for additional funds for the program. George Wiley, leader of the National Welfare Rights Organization (NWRO), remained vocally opposed to the FAP; the NWRO's organizing slogan became "Zap FAP!" The NWRO's objection to FAP was confusing on its face, given the organization's long-standing demand for a guaranteed minimum income for all Americans. However, as Steensland explains, NWRO's rejection stemmed from a deep mistrust of Nixon's motives combined with a belief that the floor set by FAP was far too low. Ultimately, then, Nixon's efforts to court African American leaders vis-à-vis the FAP failed.

Nixon understood the national frustration with welfare and the desire for reform expressed by the public in the opinion polls that he and his staff pored over. The surveys were more than ratified by the letters received by the White House, in which the public expressed almost uniform dissatisfaction with the existing regime (though for different reasons) and a strong endorsements of Nixon's early pledge to reduce aid to the nonworking poor. In some rare cases, criticism was so intense that letter writers were calling for the abolition of any but the most limited form of public assistance. Generally, though, the criticism was directed specifically at the failures of the existing system to honestly and effectively distribute aid, combat poverty, and "reform" welfare recipients themselves; and at the "unfairness" of a redistributive system that in effect took the wages of financially insecure working people and gave them to nonworking people in the form of a handout.

Bruce Blackmon was a physician and member of the North Carolina welfare board. He wrote to Nixon to let him know that while neither he nor the president "ever wants to see a human being who is in need go hungry or get cold," the whole system was out of control and had to be reined in:

> As we now get into the third generation of welfare recipients in the same families, it becomes obvious that the approach taken to date has not been successful." [We need reforms that] stop or greatly reduce illegitimate births," [and] "a change in philosophy from subsidizing status quo and procreation to a philosophy of rehabilitation and a strong positive effort to break the poverty cycle.[87] (Buies Creek, N.C., Jan. 28, 1969)

The idea that welfare had become a self-perpetuating form of dependency animated much of the criticism of federal support for the poor. The "tangle of pathology" of which Moynihan spoke in his infamous report on the black family was evident to the ordinary people who contacted the White House. A letter penned by Mrs. Hanson, who wrote to Daniel Moynihan from Junction City, Kansas, was fairly typical of what the White House received. She lambasted welfare recipients for not looking hard enough for work and for using their resources on luxuries that working people denied to themselves: "Each day you read hundreds of advertisements in the newspaper of employers asking for help," she notes, "and each day those on welfare just sit and accept what is <u>Handed Out</u> to them" (emphasis in original). Aside from "some of the aged and of course our children," she thought recipients were generally undeserving and welfare was "used for liquor, cars and many other unnecessary things."[88]

A New Mexico woman offers the same grab bag of complaints, ranging from the dubious morality of recipients to their unacceptable parenting practices and their joy at draining the coffers of hardworking people. "It is well recognized that you don't want to violate [welfare recipients'] right to be adulterous at the taxpayers expense—nor their right to rear their children in ways of corruption—quite as much as it is wished to violate the rights of working, producing, nonrioting, non-arsonistic citizens."

> And you—who are much smarter than myself—believe that money is the solution to everything—so as long as the workers can be kept down enough to take it from them. How much time during the workday is allowed by the myriads of social agencies in DC to polish all the halos worn by all the great humanitarians?

The letter closes with a warning: "I am joining a Tax-Action Group and paying for others to join so you might begin to scale down your ideas a trifle—we can also rebel and maybe even riot, if we must do so to protect our own."[89]

Urban rioters and welfare recipients might both have been colored black in the public imagination, but they were also, like student protestors and "great humanitarians," associated with the liberal political establishment that was the target of the conservative, "middle American" backlash of the period. Hence, welfare policy was tied to affirmative action, another favored target of anti-liberalism. Joseph Carbo, from Cornwells Heights, Pennsylvania, wrote to White House aide John Ehrlichman to complain about the way special privileges for minorities were creating a crisis of under qualification:

> Our nation is engaged in a mad struggle to lower all standards for the sake of its black minority. Were the millions of non-black immigrants to our cities afforded the same consideration? How can our country increase its economic productivity to meet foreign competition when we are consciously lowering employment and educational standards? Will the EEOC tell the Rand Corp. and Bell Labs that 10% of its thinkers and scientists must be black?[90] (Feb. 2, 1972)

The ecological moment was dawning in the United States during this period, with its attendant concerns about overpopulation and the need to control growth to avoid overburdening the planet. In this context, the profligacy of welfare recipients arises again and again in the White House files.

> We are faced with an over-population problem and you are doing everything to encourage people to have more children. . . . It seems rather unfair that single persons and people with one or two dependents must pay and pay for the large uncontrolled families which subsist on welfare and handouts caused mainly by just plain too many children.[91] (Letter to Moynihan from D. L. Millroy, Hollywood, Fla., Feb. 4, 1969)

> Since your [sic] delving for root causes [of poverty, welfare dependency] may I suggest a nationwide vasectomy and hysterectomy program. If you can't feed and care for your offspring—don't have them.[92] (Letter to John Ehrlichman from Mrs. Chas Stephens, Cleveland, Mo., Oct. 5, 1971)

Their only talent appears to be an ability to proliferate in numbers."[93] (Letter to Ehrlichman from Joseph L. Carbo, Cornwells
Heights, Penn., Feb. 2, 1972)

They are prolific in production—perhaps because it increases income and problems and sympathy. I note those demanding more
are those with up to 14 children or more.[94] (Mrs. J.F. Landis, Las
Cruces, N.M., May 20, 1969)

A registered nurse wrote in, "'Get me on welfare.' This remark
I've heard for 2 years, coming from unwed pregnant 13 to 18 years
olds." She continues, "After delivery, the first question and thought
is ADC, compounded by the refusal after delivering 2nd & 3rd child
to accept or try any form of birth control.[95] Often these comments
were joined by derisive attitudes about welfare recipients' abilities
as parents. "I too think the welfare plan should be changed," argued
Mrs. Sherman in a letter to Congressman Whaley.

I do believe however that the able bodied fathers are the ones that
should be brought out of the pool halls and taverns and put to
work.[96] (McVeytown, Penn., Oct. 13, 1969)

There are some people who do not have the common sense to
prevent their children from using lead paint as a meal.[97] (Letter
to Ehrlichman from Joseph L. Carbo, Cornwells Heights, Penn.,
Feb. 2, 1972)

Many times the children reap no benefits from the Aid to Dependent Children or the Welfare that is received.[98] (Mrs. John C.
Hanson, Junction City, Kan., Feb. 5, 1969)

In the meantime the psychiatrists and social workers shed crocodile
tears over the poor parents who are pressured to the point of no return by these vicious infants who invaded their homes. [99](Mrs. J.F.
Landis, Las Cruces, N.M., May 20, 1969)

A new theme developed in the Nixon era that, for the first time, identified the persistence of poverty from mother to daughter and father to son as a national scandal. The culprit here was morally misguided parents whose bad habits were aided and abetted by a social welfare system that reinforced their most deplorable qualities. Jim DeLapa from the Michigan heartland exemplifies this perspective. He describes himself as "a hard working, honest, dedicated man with a lovely wife and 4 beautiful children" and goes on to explain that the system "lends itself to the demoralization of honest people . . . leads to the loss of one's self-esteem and respect, which is further complicated by a loss of pride and initiative."

> When we have a significant number of people wanting something for nothing (and our numbers seem to be growing by over-whelming proportions) then we will have internal strife and decay. . . . Promising more of the same to the second and third generation welfare recipients just compounds the problem. Can't you see this?

Mr. DeLapa sees a stark contrast between his father's experience of poverty in the 1930s and the comparatively comfortable lives of welfare recipients in his own time. In the Depression, DeLapa relates, the going was very rough. But his father survived on his own, without help from anyone, and if anything, the hardship had strengthened him.

> Yes, old pop was indeed demoralized. But he knew that America was the land of opportunity and thru a continuation of hard work and dedication of efforts we would somehow "make it." Yes, we survived and without any form of outside help or welfare. This experience has helped thousands of poor families, like ours, to build character and add back-bone to the foundation of this country. It was thrust upon us and we were not dependant upon a hand out.[100] (Coloma, Mich., Jan. 5, 1971)

These refrains were most commonly expressed by middle- and working-class taxpayers who resented the nonworking poor, but welfare recipients themselves did not disagree. Nixon and Moynihan heard from them in the mail as well, and their comments about the need to do away with "welfare as we know it" are striking for the way they reveal a common culture, bound by the work ethic, regardless of individual circumstance. One "graduate or former beneficiary of the ADC" wrote to Moynihan, saying, "It goes without saying that many improvements have been made in the welfare and ADC systems, but nowhere does individual initiative get the recognition it deserves." Reforming the system "would provide some means for rewarding the unfortunate individual on relief who has enough initiative and self respect to work."

> Unfortunately, the present system of welfare seems to create dependency rather than help an individual to stand on his own two feet. Many of us have needed a crutch from time to time but the present system seems to consign many to a wheelchair.[101] (Letter from R. L. Smith, Burlington, Mass., Feb. 5, 1969)

Another letter, written by a member of a community group "composed solely of welfare recipients," speaks eloquently of "how much welfare limits us and kills our ability to do for ourselves. . . . Our men have lost their sense of aggression, and being a man who has lived with this handicap I know how hard it is for them to compete in this competitive society."[102] A similar commentary from a group of "lower income people and welfare recipients" in Utah begins with a complaint about how people on public assistance are unfairly stigmatized: "We are getting rather tired of hearing people say how lazy and no-account we are," the group writes.

> If we are only allowed to go and work for a wage and be a something instead of a nothing the rest of our lives because things went wrong for us and we ended up on welfare through circumstances beyond our control we could become worthwhile citizens to ourselves, our community, our state and most of all our families . . . give us the chance we need to better ourselves and help our communities, our state, our country, plus help our families to be more worthwhile citizens and realize they are better off doing for themselves rather

than sitting home letting someone else support them.[103] (Letter from eleven Utah residents, May 13, 1969)

Given the desire of welfare recipients to be self-reliant, and the widespread sentiment that "anything is better than the welfare mess we are in at present,"[104] it is no wonder that Nixon's FAP did not survive to the end of the legislative process. Instead, opposition to the guaranteed income idea mounted steadily. Opinion was divided even within Nixon's inner circle. While Moynihan was a major proponent (and draftsman) of the plan, Arthur Burns, chairman of the Federal Reserve, was its most vociferous critic. In late April he sent Nixon the results of a Gallup poll that asked respondents whether they would "favor or oppose" a guaranteed income plan of "at least $3,200 a year." Opposition was strong and growing from June 1968 to January 1969 overall, for whites and across all but the lowest income bracket.[105]

But for most Americans, the very idea of a guaranteed income floor was an anathema. By the summer of 1972, fully 73% of the public opposed the idea. Earlier surveys suggest that the most popular reason for objecting to guaranteed income, endorsed by 53% of respondents who explained their opposition, was that it would "destroy initiative," while others thought the program smacked of either socialism (7%) or communism (2%).

The guarantee represented another work disincentive and discouraged ambition and independence. "There certainly are people who are in need of temporary assistance," wrote Eleanor Garrett of Huntington, New York," but guaranteeing people a basic amount of income would seem to me to be a sure way of stifling ambition, ingenuity and incentive. One of the basic theories of capitalism is competition; this stipend would destroy the stimulus that competition offers."[106]

A woman who identified herself as chairman of the "Welfare Study Committee of the Macomb County Homeowners and Taxpayers Association," writing on behalf of the same, said:

We do not agree with a $5,400 guaranteed annual income for welfare families, which was recently proposed. This is more than $100

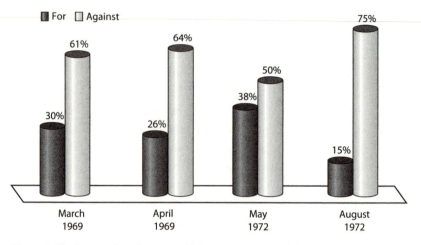

Figure 2.11. Support for a Guaranteed Minimum Income, 1969–1972
Sources: Gallup 1969, May 1972; Louis Harris & Associates, August 1972

weekly and tax free, which is more than the average working person brings home. We feel we are working for what we have and welfare recipients are not entitled to the same, if they do not work for it.[107] (Doris L. Picard to Nixon, Warren, Mich., June 12, 1969)

At times, Nixon's advisors were chided for the president's naïve belief in the character of workers who would be eligible for FAP funds. He was being duped into thinking that recipients were honorable people who just needed a little boost. Instead, they would take him to the cleaners. Eugene Tinker, a resident of Jamaica, in the borough of Queens, New York, wrote to John Ehrlichman and urged him to set President Nixon straight on the kind of people he was trying to help with the FAP plan.

Mr. Ehrlichman, the President has been led to believe that the indigent, the slothful (and other types) will gradually react with the same sincerity which he has always experienced. They will not respect the concept as now proposed! Instead, the way is being paved for a destructive series of future "give-aways" that no society can support! . . . Millions of the "below-par" adults simply do not understand or share the President's sincerity of purpose. They simply

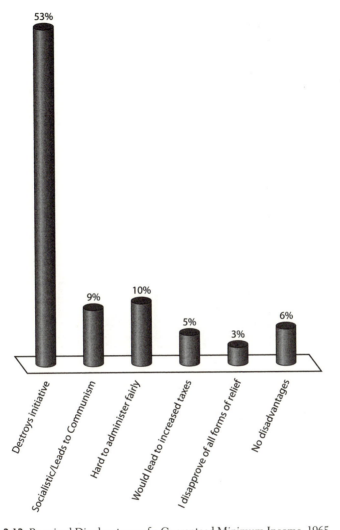

53%

9% 10%

5%

3%

6%

Destroys initiative

Socialistic/Leads to Communism

Hard to administer fairly

Would lead to increased taxes

I disapprove of all forms of relief

No disadvantages

Figure 2.12. Perceived Disadvantages of a Guaranteed Minimum Income, 1965
Source: Gallup, 1965

<u>WANT</u> . . . without qualifying for increased earnings. Many of them think very little . . . nor are they trying to learn. (Mar. 31, 1970; emphasis in the original)[108]

One woman wrote, "a guaranteed annual income for heads of families in need is the most preposterous thought to come along in this

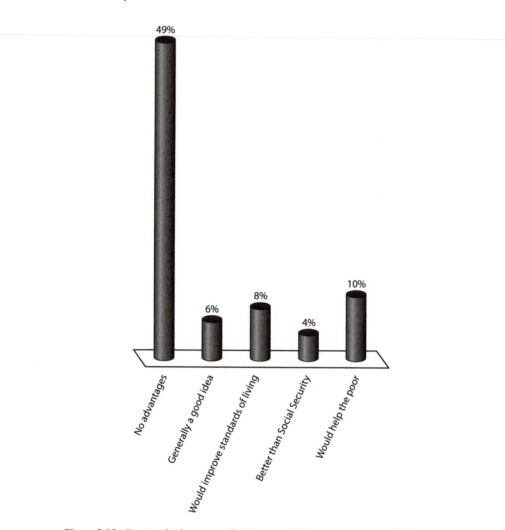

Figure 2.13. Perceived Advantages of a Guaranteed Minimum Income, 1965
Source: Gallup, 1965

decade. . . . I'm tired of working for someone else's 'free ride,' then being penalized thru taxes for not asking anyone for anything. Guaranteed income—NO. A job that contributes guaranteed income if you produce—YES."[109]

Citizens criticized the guaranteed income plan for increasing the welfare rolls at a time when it already seemed to many that the rolls were filled to overflowing and becoming and unbearable burden to taxpayers and local governments. Others argued that the money would be wasted. "In a way it isn't fair to the welfare recipient to give cash because . . . most are childlike, having no discipline and no ability to manage money. Even with an enormous daily income the children of these people would still be hungry. Annual income in cash would be like pouring water into a sieve, producing good for no one. . . . From daily observations at the grass-root level, the annual cash income for welfare recipients would be a boondoggle of the first water—complete waste."[110]

The guaranteed income plan was also criticized roundly in communications sent to the White House from the business community, particularly those from trade groups like the Chamber of Commerce (one of the loudest and most frequent critics of the FAP) and some small-business owners who shared the Burgher mentality about the poor of middle-class letter writers.

Businessmen were particularly wary of Nixon's plan to incorporate the "working poor." They pointed to the now familiar concerns that it would discourage the work ethic and exacerbate dependency on handouts. "They have their cigarette and drink money and NEED no more work than that," explained John Fandrick, owner of Fandrick Farm Supply. "Instead of supplementing this lifestyle, he wanted reform that would "let able earn their bread. . . . These people need work, but as long as some one will feed them without it, they won't work, except for incidentals."[111]

The president of Western Maintenance Company was "astounded and disturbed by a proposal recently brought to our attention, under which federal money would be provided to supplement the income of fathers who work but don't earn enough to support their families."

> We firmly believe that this sort of thing would be one more step in the wrong direction—that we have had too much of this sort of thing too long—and that it is time to allow free enterprise to see what it can do about some of the nation's economic problems. . . .
> [I]t would be a great error to take away from any man the opportunity to work out the solutions to his own problems—we believe that

adversity can bring out the best qualities in mankind.[112] (William K. Phillips to Moynihan, Santa Barbara, Calif., May 20, 1969)

Another concerned businessman who was a member of his local Chamber of Commerce wrote "to support that kind of program which will benefit deserving welfare recipients without overtaxing those who are called upon to finance said program. We recognize that one serious condition raising havoc with today's socio-economic structure is the difficulty in teaching the 'work concept' to many on the welfare rolls." The Chamber recommends "welfare reform which would make it mandatory that welfare recipients who are able to, perform an <u>act of work</u> for earning this financial assistance" and does not support "a 'Guaranteed Income' welfare program because it tends to destroy the individual's incentive to improve his capabilities as a worker."[113]

Buried in the avalanche of correspondence from small-business owners around the country is a batch of letters that arrived in May 1969 in what appears to have been a coordinated letter-writing campaign orchestrated by a trade group representing building service contractors. The contractors revealed their real objection: that providing a guaranteed income for the working poor would remove the incentive for them to take a second job to make ends meet. These firms relied on a "moonlighting" labor force, and anything that removed the urgency to work a second shift would hit them in the pocketbook.

The president of the National Association of Building Service Contractors wrote to say that while his industry supported efforts to "alleviate the economic hardship of low-income families," it was equally important to "keep the economy virile by offering opportunities for workers to support themselves in dignity." An income supplement would "kill work incentives and cause severe economic repercussions—an inflation spiral, the crippling of industries such as our own where the companies are dependent upon 'moonlighters' for their source of labor. . . . Why wouldn't a subsidy be more appealing to this group than expending the energy to work for extra money to supply family needs?"[114]

In the weeks that followed, affiliated groups and firms wrote similar letters to the White House. The president of the Association of Contract Cleaners of St. Louis wrote that "if this proposal to subsidize fathers who work full-time but don't earn enough to support their families would be passed, it would severely cripple the contract cleaning industry. . . . This proposed subsidy would destroy the incentive to work to supplement incomes derived from full-time day jobs."[115]

The secretary of Work-Master, Inc., wrote, "such a subsidy would tend to destroy the incentive and ambition of the individual on which these programs are supposed to capitalize and develop." Doing so "would severely reduce the incentive to work on an extra job; cripple the building service industry; and lastly, but far from being least in importance, derogate the pride and self-respect now held by individuals at a time when much money is being expended elsewhere to assist them in bettering their lot."[116]

Arch Booth, executive vice-president of the Chamber of Commerce, explained the chamber's opposition in a letter to Nixon. "As to the 3,000,000 families with fully-employed fathers, which would be added to the welfare rolls, we believe that they, too, should be given opportunities to equip themselves for better paying jobs. But we do not believe that adding them to the welfare rolls is a solution to the basic welfare problem. . . . We believe that work incentives and personal initiative would be weakened by such a program. . . . We believe that in its total effect, this part of the program—paying welfare to fully-employed father families—would impair the nation's productivity."[117]

In their classic *Regulating the Poor,* Frances Fox Piven and Richard Cloward made the point many years ago that the restrictive and expansive cycles of welfare reform should be stood as accordion-like instruments of social control over the "reserve army of the unemployed." They argued that when "mass unemployment leads to outbreaks of turmoil, relief programs are ordinarily initiated or expanded to absorb and control enough of the unemployed to restore order; then, as turbulence subsides, the relief system contracts, expelling those who are needed to populate the labor market."[118] The state closes the doors of social policy when capitalists need to drive those at the bottom into the labor force and opens them (marginally, perhaps) when labor markets are loose. The history of the FAP offers a complex amendment to their argument. At 3.6%, the unemployment rate was low when the White House put the FAP forward to Congress, but the political pressures building up behind the AFDC system were reaching a crescendo. Nixon intended to pull the poor into the labor market by increasing the incentives for work, while punishing those who remained on the dole.

At the same time, the FAP promised greater economic stability and a higher standard of living to the poor than anything proposed before. For firms that depended on this labor as primary employers, FAP was a huge subsidy and hence increased the prospect of a captive labor force at the taxpayer's expense. But as the letters in this section demonstrate, FAP lifted the pressure poor workers were under to tie themselves to a secondary labor market of "overtime jobs." The employers who relied on this second shift knew they would be in trouble and did what they could to block the plan. These two segments of the employer world were at odds with each other, and neither was particularly enthusiastic about the extension of wage subsidies to the working poor, much as they both applauded the work requirements of the FAP that fit, to a "T," the restrictive cycle first outlined in *Regulating the Poor*.

In the end, the FAP passed the House twice but was removed from the welfare reform bill that finally passed the Senate in October 1972. The plan was a casualty of the struggle between liberals' desire for an affordable standard of living and "fair" work requirements and conservatives' fears of budget-busting programs, with the final no vote representing an unlikely coalition of conservative, liberal, and reactionary senators. Nonetheless, the idea survives in a somewhat more limited form in the Earned Income Tax Credit, which was proposed by Senator Russell Long in 1975 and made permanent in 1978.[119] We do not mean to suggest that the EITC is a lineal descendant of the ill-fated FAP. But as Brian Steensland has pointed out, the effort to place an income floor under working families though a substantial tax rebate (effectively a wage subsidy) bears a family resemblance to

FAP, though it is clearly far more targeted in that it is available to working families only, rather than the broad coverage envisioned by Nixon.[120] Hence, even when political leaders face a headwind that defeats them, as was clearly the case here, their efforts may soften up the country for progressive measures in the years to come, merely by raising the issue and advancing solution.

THE CONTINUITY OF AMBIVALENCE

If we remember both the 1930s and the 1960s as periods of progressive change, measured by dramatic increases in state support of those at the bottom of the social structure, we must temper the memory by recognizing how unevenly they were greeted by citizens. Despite the desperate conditions of the Great Depression, we see significant pushback even in states where the unemployment rate was catastrophically high.

The Johnson era was a period of tremendous prosperity; hence, widespread hardship was not the impetus for the Great Society. Instead, shame at the condition of the poor in the midst of wealth motivated a new crusade. The general public did not particularly share in the embarrassment. Indeed, ending poverty ranked relatively low in the public's sense of important changes they wanted to see in the world—just 9% saw ridding the world of poverty as the most important goal, compared to 31% who wanted to "get all men to believe in God." It was the elite policymakers who rose to the challenge and urged the country to follow.

Rising welfare rolls spurred the Nixon administration to action. If their goals had been the simple reduction of the fiscal burden on the state and the taxpayer, the Nixonites could have embarked on a path more like the one followed years later by the Clinton administration, which created time limits to public assistance. That is not what Nixon was after; his FAP would have provided a (low) guaranteed minimum income to all Americans, indefinitely. Although his plan did not survive the legislative process, it introduced the idea of a negative income tax into the public sphere. Today, the EITC reflects the essence of this negative income tax idea—albeit for a particular

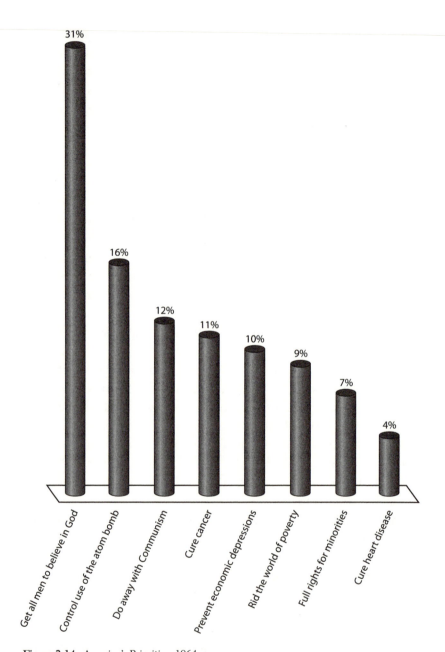

31%

16%

12%
11%
10%
9%
7%
4%

Get all men to believe in God

Control use of the atom bomb

Do away with Communism

Cure cancer

Prevent economic depressions

Rid the world of poverty

Full rights for minorities

Cure heart disease

Figure 2.14. America's Priorities, 1964
Note: Respondents were asked to answer the question: "What is the most important thing
that you would like to see happen?" Categories reflect the original Harris Poll phrasing.
Source: Louis Harris & Associates, 1964.

subset of low income families—in its delivery of a wage subsidy to poor workers.

The continuity with the 1930s is clear enough: Americans were more readily willing to extend government's helping hand to the poor who were in the labor market than to the able-bodied standing outside it. We are, in this sense, the keeper of some brothers, but hardly all. And judging from the opinion polls of the time, American sympathies for the working poor extended to wage subsidies of the kind that are provided through the EITC, and not far enough to *guarantee* a reasonable standard of living, which is what Nixon was after.

3 Economic Anxiety in the New Gilded Age

Income inequality is on the rise. The rich are getting better at passing their advantages on to their kids. Lifestyle and values gaps are widening between the educated and uneducated. So the big issue is: Will Americans demand new policies to reverse these trends—to redistribute wealth, to provide greater economic security? Are we about to see a mass populist movement in this country?

—*New York Times* columnist David Brooks[1]

As I've often said, this [income inequality] is not the type of thing which a democratic society—a capitalist democratic society—can really accept without addressing.

—Former chairman of the Federal Reserve Alan Greenspan[2]

There's no American Dream anymore.

—Jean Reynolds, age 51[3]

Jean Reynolds works full-time as a certified nursing assistant and supports three children and four grandchildren on her $1,200 per month salary. Despite spending her days working in health care, Jean has no health insurance. One of her daughters is terminally ill, and the Reynolds family faces eviction as Jean must decide between paying the rent and purchasing her daughter's prescription medication. Jean works hard, and she sees little payoff for her efforts. The American dream—the belief that hard work leads to a secure, comfortable life—has slipped from her grasp, even though she has played by the rules.

Steven Schwarzman, a cofounder of the private equity firm the Blackstone Group, is an "unabashed economic royalist" who lives in a $30 million New York City apartment once inhabited by John D. Rockefeller. Yet, like Jean Reynolds, he worries about the state of the American economy. "The middle class in the U.S. hasn't done as well over the last twenty years as people at the high end, and I think part of the compact in America is everybody has got to do better." Both conservative David Brooks and liberal Paul Krugman have worried about the future of the U.S. economy on the opinion pages of the *New York Times*. Former Federal Reserve chair Alan Greenspan, the voice of conventional wisdom, has expressed concern, as has current Federal Reserve chair Ben Bernanke.[4]

What happened over the past thirty years to unify the concerns of such disparate voices? The rise of the conservative movement and the political dominance of the Republican Party led some to believe that the country's national mood has shifted "right." For instance, one election post-mortem in the *New York Times* declared, "It is impossible to read President Bush's re-election with larger Republican majorities in both houses of Congress as anything other than the clearest confirmation yet that this is a center-right country—divided yes, but with an undisputed majority united behind his leadership."[5]

Yet the opinions expressed by Jean Reynolds, Alan Greenspan, and others are not unique. As we shall see in this chapter, decades of conservative politics and policy have pushed Americans to a breaking point. A recent survey from the Pew Research Center for the People and the Press reports that "a growing share of the public has come to agree with the view that American society is divided into two groups, the 'haves' and the 'have-nots.'" In 1988, just 26% saw a divided nation. By 2007, nearly half (48%) believed that America is a divided society. The number of Americans who see themselves as among the have-nots has doubled over the past two decades, from 17% in 1988 to 34% in 2008. Basic notions of fairness and collective responsibility have been violated.[6]

What does this broken social compact mean for American attitudes toward social welfare policies? The nation is hungry for remedies, because the current economic landscape is viewed as tilting heavily in favor of the wealthy at the expense of the working person. Even before the economic collapse of late 2008, support for a government safety net was at its highest point in many years, with roughly seven in ten Americans (69%) believing the government has a responsibility "to take care of people who can't take care of themselves." By a wide margin, Americans believe the government should guarantee "every citizen enough to eat and a place to sleep," and the proportion who share this conviction has increased markedly since the mid-1990s, when survey researchers began asking about it. In 2007, 54% believed the government should expand aid for the needy "even if it means going deeper in debt," a sharp increase over the 41% who held that view in 1994. And while a strong majority (69%) still believes that "poor people have become too dependent on government assistance programs," that figure has declined sharply over time, down from a peak of 85% in the mid-1990s.

To be sure, Americans are not marching in the streets demanding a Scandinavian-style social welfare system. We continue to place sharp limits on government intervention in the economy and still draw bright lines between the "deserving" and "undeserving" poor, just as our forebears did in the 1930s. Yet public opinion data suggest that the status quo has strained everyday Americans' tolerance for inequality and instability. Although the political party in power for most of the last twenty-five years rejected this perspective, Americans are more likely now than in the past to want government to do something to close these gaps.

Rising Inequality: The New Gilded Age

Television shows and movies have long glorified the glamorous lives of the superrich, yet most Americans have only a hazy grasp of income distribution in the United States. News anchor Charlie Gibson provided a case in point when he suggested that a family of two professors at a New Hampshire college would be "in the $200,000 range."[7] According to the Bureau of Labor Statistics, the median salary for a post-secondary educator was just over $56,000 in 2006, meaning that the "typical" family with two professors would be earning $112,000, just over half what Mr. Gibson suggested. That puts them well ahead of the average American family, that is, those in the middle fifth of the income distribution, where annual incomes are pegged at about $48,000.[8] The average income of those in the bottom fifth is just over $11,000. An entirely different set of numbers tells the story of the top earners. Median income for individuals in the top 5% of the distribution was about $189,000; the top 1% pockets $385,000. And way up in the stratosphere, where we find the top 0.1%, annual income was a whopping $2,500,000.[9]

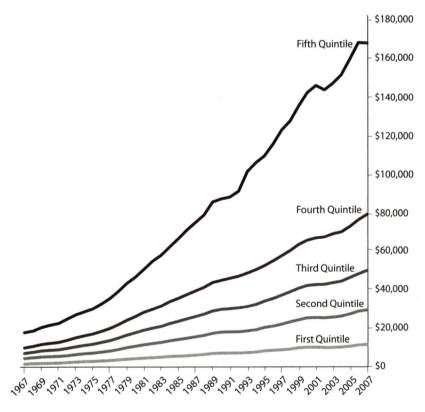

Figure 3.1. Average Household Income by Quintile, 1967–2007
Note: Income is in 2008 dollars. 1967 incomes by quintile are: first, $1,600; second, $4,433; third, $7,077; fourth, $9,902; and fifth, $17,820.
Source: U.S. Census Historical Income Tables, H-3

Over the last three decades, the American economy has become both vastly richer and vastly more unequal, as the spoils of economic growth buoyed the fortunes of those at the top while doing relatively little for the remainder of the nation. Rising tides lifted the yachts, but did very little for the rowboats. True, after-tax income grew for everyone. But the rate of change was a steep incline for those at the top and barely noticeable for those in the bottom half. Between 1979 and 2006, middle-class incomes grew by 21%, but those in the highest quintile saw an 80% increase. And when we look at the superrich, people in the top 1% of income earners, we see a whopping 228% increase in annual income. These differences are starkest when we think of them in dollar terms. At the bottom of the income distribution, families saw an extra $900 over the course of 27 years. The middle pocketed $8,700. The top 1% reaped a huge windfall of $745,000.

Rising inequality has not always been a prominent feature of the American economy. Indeed, economic inequality fell during the 1930s and 1940s in what economists Claudia Goldin and Robert Margo have termed "the Great Compression."[10] Wages narrowed by

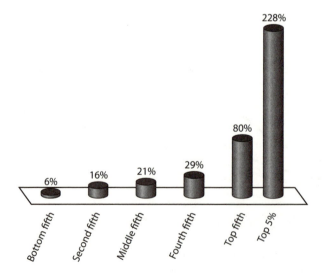

Figure 3.2. Growth in Household Post-Tax Income, 1979–2005
Source: Congressional Budget Office, December 2007

education, job experience, region, and occupation. The post-war era of shared prosperity saw economic growth fairly evenly distributed in U.S. society. From the late 1940s through the mid-1970s, the real incomes of working poor families[11] and affluent families[12] both grew by 98%. Income growth was slightly higher for middle-class families and slightly lower for those in the 95th percentile, but every income group experienced real income growth of between 2.4% and 2.7% per year.

Prominent economists thought that growth, coupled with decreasing economic disparities, was a hallmark of advanced postindustrial societies. Perhaps most famous was Simon Kuznets, who introduced the concept of the Kuznets curve, an inverted U-shaped curve resulting from plotting inequality against income per capita. Kuznets hypothesized that as countries transitioned from an agrarian economy to an industrial economy, both per capita income and income inequality would grow. The transition from an industrial to a post-industrial economy was supposed to be accompanied by growth in per capita income and a decline in inequality, due to rising educational opportunity and increased government efforts at redistribution.

Kuznets's theory flopped. Instead of shared prosperity, rising economic inequality has become an enduring feature of the contemporary American economy. Wage and income inequality have continued to grow through both economic expansions and contractions. If each quintile represents a rung on a ladder, the space between each rung has grown farther and farther apart since the 1970s.

Perhaps even more striking, the space between the rungs at the very top of the ladder has spread out. Economists Emmanuel Saez and Thomas Piketty's careful examination of incomes at the top of the distribution suggests that real incomes for those in the top 0.01th percentile have grown dramatically faster even than those very privileged people just a bit below them on the ladder. Between 1926 and 2006, incomes for those in the 99.99th percentile grew by nearly 360%, compared to "just" 279% for those in the 95th percentile. This "growing apart" began in the 1970s, accelerated in the 1980s, and, with the exception of a relatively small blip due to the bursting of the technology bubble in the early 2000s, has continued apace to date.[13]

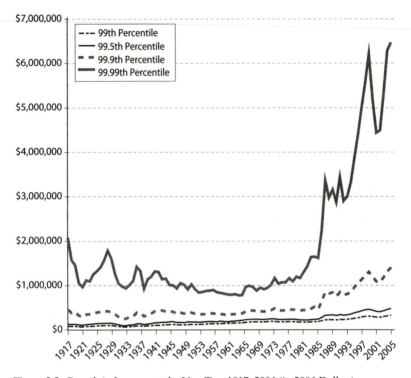

Figure 3.3. Growth in Incomes at the Very Top, 1917–2006 (in 2006 Dollars)
Source: Emmanuel Saez's computations from IRS income tax statistics, http://elsa.berkeley
.edu/~saez

The Forbes 400, a list of America's wealthiest 400 individuals, provides an apt example of the skyrocketing fortunes of the über-rich.
According to a *New York Times* story on the subject, twenty years
ago there were fourteen American billionaires on the list. Today, the
Forbes 400 includes 374 known billionaires. In 2005, the 400 richest
people in America were worth more than the gross domestic product
of Canada, and more than the *combined* gross domestic product of
Switzerland, Poland, Norway, and Greece.

   Further evidence of the income explosion at the top of the ladder
comes from studies of CEO pay. Economists Carola Frydman and
Raven Saks looked at the earnings of top executives from the 1930s
through the present.[14] They discovered that after three decades of

modest growth following the Second World War, executive compensation shot through the roof beginning in the 1980s. Between 1995 and 1999, CEO pay reached an average growth rate of more then 10% a year, and the exponential growth in pay continued following the collapse of the stock market boom in the early 2000s. In 2005, a CEO earned 262 times the pay of the average worker. In other words, the average CEO earned more in one workday than the average worker earned in a year.

New York Times business reporter Louis Uchitelle refers to the contemporary era as "the New Gilded Age," an apt description for a period characterized by a dense concentration of wealth at the top.[15] Only twice before over the last century has 5% of the national income gone to those in the upper one one-hundredth of a percent of the income distribution—in 1915, when the original Gilded Age was coming to a close, and in the late 1920s, before the stock market crash. Both of those periods closed with the election of progressive governments (Woodrow Wilson in 1912 and Roosevelt in the 1930s), which should give us a hint about how hard it has been historically for Americans to swallow these vast gaps.

Evaluating the New Gilded Age:
Public Opinion on Inequality

The rise in economic inequality in the United States presents a puzzle for students of the American economy. What explains this tectonic shift in the distribution of income? Most accounts fit well within the classic economic framework of supply and demand. For instance, an early consensus formed around the idea of "skills-biased technological change" as the leading culprit.[16] Wages make up the vast majority of most American families' total incomes; therefore, explaining inequality of that kind could go quite a way toward explaining the gap in total family incomes between the rich and the rest. The argument behind skills-biased technological change is straightforward: technological advances led to a rise in the demand for skilled workers, thus the wage premium for skilled workers grew more quickly than did the wage premium for less skilled workers. The result is a labor market characterized by highly unequal wages.

Ten years later, however, this argument looked less promising, as inequality among workers with similar educational backgrounds, and therefore similar skill sets, continued to grow. A variety of other common explanations foundered as well. For instance, globalization might explain part of the decline in the median wage, but it does little to explain the explosive growth in CEO pay. Economists Robert H. Frank and Phillip Cook's compelling "winner-take-all" theory argued that when millions have an interest in the winner's performance, a large reward goes to that winner.[17] As the market becomes oversaturated with aspiring superstars, the inevitable multitude of losers are left with little reward for their effort. The "winner-take-all" theory might explain Michael Jordan's salary, but what of all the billionaires who can't dunk? Economists began rummaging in new toolboxes for explanations of another kind.

Perhaps, some thought, *social norms* could explain the run-up in inequality. Conventional wisdom suggested that the "Greatest Generation," Americans who came of age during the halcyon days following the end of the Second World War, held strong norms of equality and fairness. If these norms eroded, the excesses of the 1980s and 1990s could be explained by the coming of age of a new generation of Americans with little regard for economic justice. The explanation appealed to many, including Nobel Laureate and *New York Times* columnist Paul Krugman, who penned a cover story for the paper's Sunday magazine wondering whether social norms weren't at the heart of the inequality explosion:

> Some—by no means all—economists trying to understand growing inequality have begun to take seriously a hypothesis that would have been considered irredeemably fuzzy-minded not long ago. This view stresses the role of social norms in setting limits to inequality. According to this view, the New Deal had a more profound impact on American society than even its most ardent admirers have suggested: it imposed norms of relative equality in pay that persisted for more than 30 years, creating the broadly middle-class society we

came to take for granted. But those norms began to unravel in the 1970's and have done so at an accelerating pace.[18]

Is Krugman right? Have the social norms bolstering the society that produced the New Deal and the Great Society unraveled over the last thirty years? The victories of the Republican Party, beginning with Ronald Reagan and continuing (with the interruption of the middle-of-the-road Clinton White House) through two Bush presidencies, might lead us to believe Krugman has got something there. Yet as we shall see shortly, public opinion data suggest otherwise. The broad social compact attributed to the New Deal and Great Society is perhaps more accurately described as the product of present-day nostalgia than as empirical fact. Americans are willing to live with substantial economic inequality, particularly when compared with other advanced economies. Yet tolerance for inequality has not increased apace with the widening gap in the income distribution. Instead, we find that American's tolerance for inequality has actually *diminished* over time.

Join the Rich, Don't Soak Them?

In 2006, the *Economist* magazine featured a story on economic inequality in America. Despite the increasing gap between the rich and the poor, the authors argued, Americans were not particularly ruffled. They explained:

> Americans do not go in for envy. The gap between rich and poor is bigger than in any other advanced country, but most people are unconcerned. Whereas Europeans fret about the way the economic pie is divided, Americans want to join the rich, not soak them. Eight out of ten, more than anywhere else, believe that though you may start poor, if you work hard, you can make pots of money. It is a central part of the American Dream.[19]

The magazine's observation that Americans want to "join the rich, not soak them" is echoed by social scientists. For instance, after reviewing American attitudes toward the wealthy, political scientists

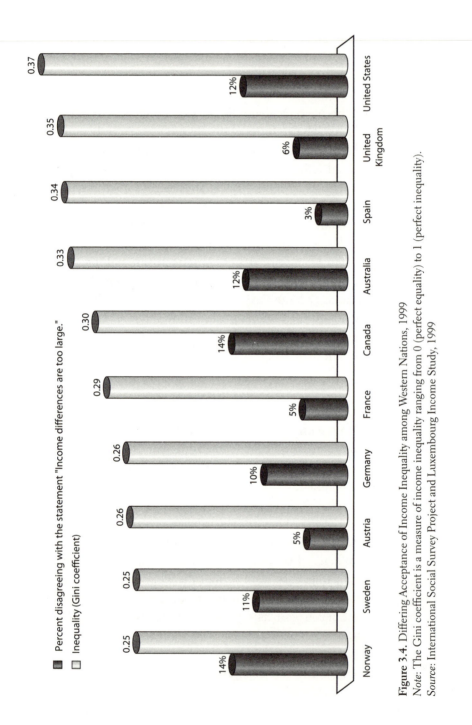

■ Percent disagreeing with the statement "Income differences are too large."

☐ Inequality (Gini coefficient)

Figure 3.4. Differing Acceptance of Income Inequality among Western Nations, 1999
Note: The Gini coefficient is a measure of income inequality ranging from 0 (perfect equality) to 1 (perfect inequality).
Source: International Social Survey Project and Luxembourg Income Study, 1999

Everett Carl Ladd and Karlyn Bowman conclude, "In general, . . . while many Americans are ambivalent about great wealth, few are hostile to it. This goes far to explain why disparities in wealth in this country have generated so little political heat."[20] Political scientist Andrew Hacker comes to a similar conclusion: "There is little evidence that Americans of modest means spend much time or energy feeling resentful toward the rich. If anything, it appears that taxpayers vent more anger toward families receiving public assistance than they do worrying about the perquisites of those with wealth."[21]

Indeed, recent survey data confirm that Americans are less concerned with inequality than are comparable European nations, particularly in light of the high levels of actual income inequality. In figure 3.4, income inequality is captured by the Gini coefficient, a commonly used measure of dispersion ranging from 0 (perfect equality, where everyone has exactly the same income) to 1 (perfect inequality, where one person has all of the income and everyone else has zero income). Inequality in the United States is the highest of all of the countries compared, at 0.37, as compared to a low of 0.25 in Norway.

Tolerance for income inequality is measured by respondents' level of agreement with the statement "Income differences in [country] are too large."[22] Individuals who either disagree or strongly disagree are "inequality-tolerant." Despite high levels of inequality in the United States, 12.4% of the American sample disagrees when asked whether inequality is too high in their country. In other words, 12.4% are inequality-tolerant. In comparison, in other high-inequality nations, inequality tolerance is far lower. In contrast, in Spain, just 3.3% of respondents are inequality tolerant. In Austria, a nation characterized by relatively low levels of inequality, tolerance for inequality is far lower than in the highly unequal United States: just 4.7% of Austrians are inequality tolerant. In short, compared to other Western nations, Americans are willing to put up with more economic inequality. Even so, an overwhelming majority of us believe income differences are too large.

Explanations for Americans' relative indifference toward economic inequality touch on the distinction between equality of opportunity and equality of outcomes, a principle that has long served as the basic underpinning of American public opinion toward economic inequality. Indeed, Alexis de Toqueville emphasized the distinction between equality of opportunity and equality of results in his nineteenth-century journeys through America.[23] Some couch this tension in the language of "democracy" versus "capitalism," whereby democracy guarantees equal opportunity and capitalism allows for differentiated results. Similarly, political scientist Stanley Feldman concludes that Americans use different principles for addressing "micro-justice" (individual rewards) versus "macro-justice" (the distribution of rewards).[24]

Jennifer Hochschild's interviews with New Haven residents in the 1970s put this tension between equality of opportunity and equality of outcomes in sharp relief.[25] Her respondents were "egalitarian in the political domain, [i.e.] they want political and civil rights to be distributed equally among all citizens," but they were more ambiguous when it came to equalizing economic outcomes. Those New Haven dwellers supported equality "as long as it is couched in terms of . . . investments" in human capital development, thereby equalizing the playing field so that all would have the opportunity to succeed. In short, Hochschild argues, in the economic domain, Americans "agree on a principle of differentiation, not equality. . . . They define political freedom as strict equality, but economic freedom as an equal chance to become unequal."

Political scientist Larry Bartels comes to much the same conclusion based on an analysis of the National Election Studies from 1984 to 2004.[26] More than 85% of respondents agreed that "our country should do whatever is necessary to make sure that everyone has an equal opportunity to succeed." As Bartels notes, the questions that reference "an equal chance" or "equal treatment" generate favorable responses from between one-half and two-thirds of all respondents. Those questions referring to "how equal people are" and "pushing equal rights" were notably less popular. "These differences suggest a consequential distinction in public thinking between equality of opportunity and equality of results," he concludes.

Compared to our European counterparts, Americans care more about achievement and opportunity than they do about equality of outcome. Even in an era of historically-high levels of economic in-

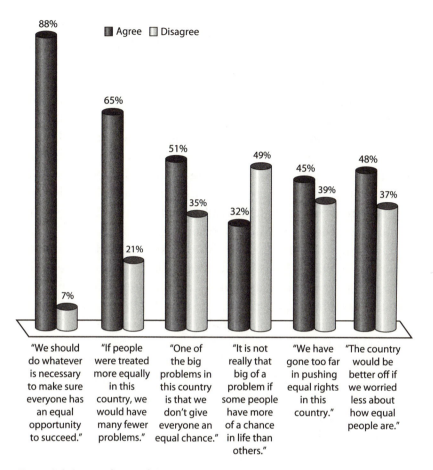

Figure 3.5. Support for Equal Opportunity in America
Source: Pooled data from the National Election Studies, 1984–2004

equality, American public opinion is relatively tepid when it comes to questions of economic justice in terms of outcomes. Give us equal opportunity, yes. But equal outcomes? We're less sure we like that idea.

Change over Time: Have Americans Become More Tolerant of Inequality?

At the heart of Krugman's social norms explanation of rising inequality is an argument about cultural change. Perhaps inequality has grown because we are more prepared to accept greater levels of economic dispersion now than we were in the past. The prior section showed that we are more tolerant of inequality than other countries. Has that sentiment been increasing?

Between the 1970s and today, many other norms have shifted dramatically. Racial prejudice has sharply diminished, and attitudes toward women's roles in society have also changed dramatically.[27] Younger generations are more accepting of gay citizens. If these norms can change, why not those that govern our views of economic inequality? Perhaps the gradual passing of the Greatest Generation means that a cohort of highly egalitarian individuals is slowly being replaced by a cohort of greedy, callous individuals with little regard for the basic contours of the American social compact?

Public opinion shows quite the opposite. Indeed, if anything, American tolerance for economic inequality has actually *decreased* across time, not increased. Younger cohorts are *less tolerant* of inequality than their grandparents. The idea that the Greatest Generation is the standard-bearer of equality should be put to rest.

Several major surveys bear out this conclusion.[28] NORC's General Social Survey (GSS) provides our most comprehensive source of data on trends in American attitudes toward economic inequality, with a set of questions asked in 1987, 1992, and 1999.[29] It is unfortunate that the series didn't begin even earlier, before inequality began to grow so rapidly. If it had, we would be able to identify a "baseline" against which to compare the historical records that have developed since. Still, the time series covers the period in which rising inequality first became widely acknowledged among academics and other experts, probably some time in the early 1990s.

One of these questions, "Are income differences in America too large?", gives us a reasonable handle on American attitudes toward inequality. The percentage of Americans who believed income inequality was too high increased between 1987 and 1992, a period of sharply rising inequality, from 58.5% percent in 1987 to 67.2%.[30] Despite the economic boom of the 1990s, the belief that inequality was too high persisted. In simple terms, as the gap between rich and poor in American yawned wider, the public became increasingly dissatisfied with the inequality they saw around them.

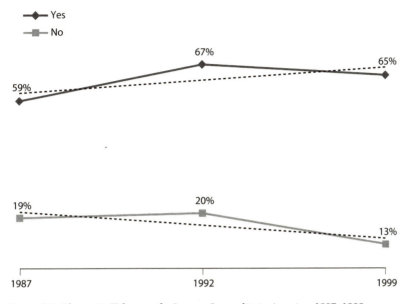

Figure 3.6. Change in Tolerance for Income Inequality in America, 1987–1999
Note: Respondents were asked to respond to the question: "Are income differences in America too large?"
Source: General Social Survey Inequality Modules I, II, and III

We can dig a little deeper by relying on another battery of questions in which respondents are asked how much money particular occupations—such as doctors, clerks, a CEO of a multinational corporation, a skilled worker, an unskilled worker, and a cabinet minister—*should* be earning. Respondents are then asked to approximate how much each of these occupations *actually* earns. When we put these two sets of responses together, we can calculate the gap between what wages *are* and what wages *should be*, with higher values representing a stronger relative concern with wage inequality.[31] We could characterize a person as "concerned" with wage inequality if his score is positive and "unconcerned" if his score is negative. Figures 3.7 and 3.8 illustrate the sharp rise in the proportion of survey respondents who are concerned about wage inequality. The line rises consistently across the time period examined, as did the proportion expressing serious concern with wage inequality.

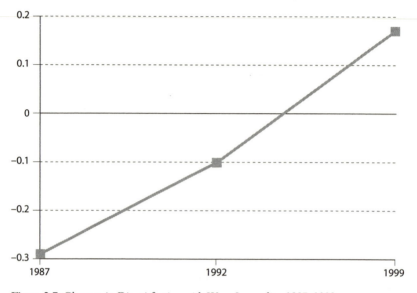

Figure 3.7. Changes in Dissatisfaction with Wage Inequality, 1987–1999
Note: Figure shows the average distance between respondents' perceived "fair" and "actual" wages, across occupation. Higher scores on this measure indicate greater dissatisfaction with wage inequality. See the text and accompanying note for a complete description of the methodology behind the computation of dissatisfaction with wage inequality.
Source: General Social Survey Inequality Modules I, II, and III

Sociologist Leslie McCall has come to the same conclusions.[32] Drawing on GSS analyses, she notes that the percentage of individuals who believe inequality continues to exist because it benefits "the rich and powerful" doubled between 1987 and 1996, from 14% to 28%. The increase in those who strongly agree that income differences are unnecessary for economic prosperity was even sharper, rising from 6% in 1987 to 26% in 1996.[33]

None of this lends support to Krugman's thesis regarding a cultural shift toward greater tolerance for a widening gap between rich and poor. Rather than growing more forgiving of income and wage disparities, Americans have become increasingly cranky about inequality. They are more likely now than in the past to believe that income differences are too large, and more likely to report a large gap between their ideal distribution of wages and their perceptions of

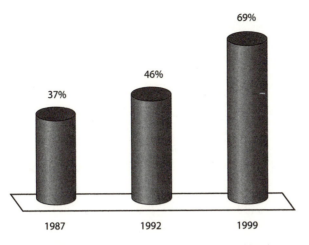

Figure 3.8. Change in Concern with Wage Inequality, 1987–1999
Note: Concern with wage inequality is represented by the average positive score on a measure capturing the difference between a respondent's perception of "actual" and "fair" wages across a range of occupations. Respondents scoring a 3 or higher on this scale are coded as agreeing that income differences in America were too large. See the text and related note for a more detailed explanation of the methodology used to construct this metric.
Source: General Social Survey Inequality Modules I, II and III

the actual distribution of wages. We are less likely to view economic inequality as an acceptable correlate of economic prosperity.

GENERATIONAL CONTINUITY

Public opinion during the New Deal era was not as generous toward the poor as we may like to remember. That may help to explain why the cohort change argument holds so little promise: the Greatest Generation is no more egalitarian than younger birth cohorts. If anything, older generations appear to be more tolerant of economic inequality than their children or grandchildren.

While people change their minds about a lot of things as they age, we know that when it comes to attitudes toward economic questions, opinions tend to crystallize around the age when respondents entered the labor market. We can speak of the "Depression Generation" or "Gen X," because the conditions these cohorts met when they tried to slot themselves into the labor market tended to shape their expectations and values.[34] To get at this kind of generational culture, we use a rough approximation of labor market entry at the age of eighteen and then divide the GSS sample into five birth cohorts.[35] Cohort 1 includes individuals born between 1905 and 1929, and comprises those who came of age during the New Deal/Second World War period. Cohort 2, born between 1930 and 1944, includes individuals who came of age during the halcyon days following the Second World War. Cohort 3, born between 1945 and 1954, turned eighteen during the 1960s, a period of tumultuous social change. Cohort 4, born between 1955 and 1969, came of age during the economic crises of the 1970s, a period characterized by "stagflation" and economic hardship. Cohort 5, born between 1970 and 1983, came of age after 1988. Today, these Americans are in their mid-twenties to late thirties, and hence experienced young adulthood during an era of conspicuous consumption and economic prosperity. Each cohort is roughly equal in size.

As figure 3.9 illustrates, the difference in attitudes toward income inequality does not vary substantially by birth cohort. All five birth cohorts express a basic degree of concern with the level of income inequality, with mean values of between 3.7 and 3.8. Regardless of when they came of age, most Americans are only somewhat concerned with income disparities in the United States. If the explanation for growing inequality lay in the increasing tolerance of new generations for big gaps between haves and have-nots, we would expect to see that the Greatest Generation, those in Cohorts 1 and 2, who came of age during the Great Depression, the Second World War, and the days of shared prosperity following the war, boast markedly more egalitarian ideals than younger birth cohorts. Instead, we see that they their share some basic assumptions with their children and grandchildren, whose economic experience was quite different.

It is not a simple task to disentangle the impact of generational experience from the simultaneous effects of age and historical period. "Age effects" refers to the relationship between age and attitudes. As individuals move through the life cycle, they change their perspective because their roles in life change. Men and women may become

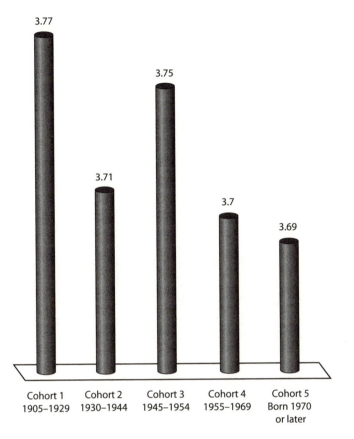

Figure 3.9. Tolerance for Income Inequality, by Birth Cohort

Note: Shown is the average level of agreement that "income differences in America are too large." Answers range from 1 (strongly agree) to 5 (strongly disagree). Respondents scoring a 3 or higher on this scale are coded as agreeing that income differences in America were too large.

Source: General Social Survey Social Inequality Modules I, II, and III (pooled sample from 1987 to 1999)

more conservative on economic questions as they take on increasing levels of financial responsibility (for their children or their aging parents), and that experience may incline them toward a less generous attitude toward those outside their family. "Period effects" simply refers to the impact of a particular moment in time. For instance, the civil rights era of the 1960s had an impact on everyone—young and old alike—who was alive to see the dramatic changes it brought about. Parsing these three related effects is a challenging task. Age effects can always be expressed as some combination of cohort and period effects, while period effects can always be expressed as some combination of cohort and age effects.

The absence of substantial variation across birth cohorts' attitudes toward income inequality suggests that generation is unlikely to be a powerful explanation for the change in attitudes toward inequality between 1987 and 1999. Nonetheless, we use a basic statistical technique that allows us to compare the relative impact of birth cohort and time period, as well as a variety of other factors that might reasonably predict attitudes toward inequality.[36] This analysis confirms that cohort effects are not significant predictors of attitudes toward inequality, and reaffirms the importance of period effects on these attitudes. The odds that an American would agree or strongly agree that "income differences are too large" in 1992 are 2.5 times greater than in 1987. In 1999, the odds of agreement slip to just over one time those on 1987. In short, birth cohort has no predictive power, and attitudes toward inequality have grown less tolerant across time (table 3.1).[37]

Table 3.1   Model Results Comparing the Impact of Birth Cohort and Period on Tolerance for Income Inequality

	Cohort 2	Cohort 3	Cohort 4	Cohort 5	1992	1999
OLS Models (ßs)						
Income	−0.017	−0.010	−0.075	−0.189	0.427***	0.163***
Inequality	(−0.06)	(−0.04)	(−0.09)	(−0.15)	(−0.01)	(−0.01)
Logit Models (Odds Ratios)						
Income Inequality:	0.805	0.830	0.753	0.542*	2.548***	1.139***
Most Concerned	(−0.22)	(−0.15)	(−0.25)	(−0.20)	(−0.08)	(−0.02)

Notes: Robust standard errors in (parentheses): * significant at 10%; ** significant at 5%; *** significant at 1%.
Reference categories are Cohort 1 and 1987. In addition to birth cohort and year, models control for income, education, subjective social class, gender, labor status (unemployed or self-employed), union membership, and skill-specificity.
Source: Data are from the General Social Survey Social Inequality Modules I, II, and III.

GOVERNMENT'S ROLE IN THE NEW GILDED AGE

If American public opinion expresses discontent with the current historic high levels of economic inequality, then we might expect support for a variety of government interventions to have become more favorable. Two different kinds of policy intervention could come into play. First, redistributive social policies might be viewed more favorably today than in the past. If the rich have more than their fair share of resources relative to the poor, redistributive policies such as higher levels of taxation for the rich might be more desirable. Second, policies that address the needs of the lower half of the income distribution might be viewed more favorably. In an era in which the wealthy can easily spend over $7 million on a diamond ring, perhaps Americans will look more favorably on policies that provide a modicum of support for the least fortunate?

Conventional wisdom suggests that answer is no. Social scientists and historians have argued that a reaction set in after the welfare rolls began to climb in the 1960s, which set off a retrenchment: public opinion turned against antipoverty policies and the goals of the New Deal and Great Society welfare states. Seen against that backdrop, the 2001 tax cuts enacted by George W. Bush's administration might be deemed the capstone of an era of opposition to government intervention in American's economic lives.

This picture is simply wrong. Rather than fundamentally turning against the welfare state and the concept of redistribution from the rich to the poor, core American attitudes toward both poverty-prevention and redistribution have remained relatively constant across time. What has changed dramatically is the *context* that surrounds these attitudes. As the consequences of high levels of economic inequality have expanded to affect an increasingly larger share of the American public, the desire for government policies aimed at "fixing" inequality's harms has expanded.

Journalists Thomas and Mary Edsall's history of American views of the welfare state is relevant here.[38] Fractures in the liberal Democratic coalition between African Americans and the white working class were evident by the late 1960s, they tell us, and contributed directly to Nixon's electoral victories in 1968 and 1972. The recessionary 1970s exacerbated these preexisting tensions: "Job displacement, loss of security, new family configurations, changing neighborhoods, dangerous streets, crime, dizzying global transformations, and rapidly intensifying competition undermined the capacity of ordinary citizens to tolerate modest sacrifices in behalf of the less well off—a tolerance essential to the implementation of liberalism."[39] Similarly, historian Michael Katz argues that worsening economic conditions activated a "psychology of scarcity" that had largely disappeared during the extended post-war period of affluence and shared growth. "As they examined the sources of their distress, looking for both villains and ways to cut public spending, ordinary Americans and their elected representatives focused on welfare and its beneficiaries," he concludes.[40]

In *Canarsie*, an interview-based study of white working- and middle-class residents of the Brooklyn neighborhood, sociologist Jonathan Reider echoes these findings. "The economy of scarcity is emotional as well as political," he concludes. Canarsie residents expressed deep resentment toward "those who enjoyed the indulgence of dependency," and their "self-denial often produces an attitude of stingy misanthropy."[41] Political sociologist Theda Skocpol argues that "universal" social welfare programs enjoy far more popularity with the public than do "clientelist programs," which offer benefits only to specific subgroups of the populations. Skocpol attributes the public backlash against the antipoverty programs of the 1960s to a feeling among the working and middle class that "they have not perceived gains to themselves from increased welfare transfers to the poor," while "rising financial burdens" erode their sense of financial security. "Universal policies that have spread costs and visibly delivered benefits across classes and races," such as Social Security and Medicare, "continued to enjoy popular support well beyond that given to programs exclusively targeting the poor."[42]

Taxes were a particularly volatile issue during the 1970s for working and middle class Americans, whose fragile hold on economic security inclined them to cast a wary eye at the costs of maintaining an expensive social welfare system. Tax revolts undermined support for

Democratic liberalism, which increasingly was perceived by many as championing an expanding government committed to imposing costly redistributive burdens. Opinion polls began to register increasing opposition to taxes and complaints about government benefits for social welfare programs that offered no direct benefits to the majority of taxpayers, and seemed ineffective at alleviating poverty or addressing its perceived social and cultural effects.

The consequences for the Democratic Party were decisive. The Edsalls conclude that, throughout the 1970s, "a growing block of once-solid working class Democratic voters, their party allegiances eroded by inflation, wage and work-rule concessions, and the threat of unemployment, no longer saw programs directed toward the poor as an integral part of the broad Democratic commitment, but as a source of personal, social, and economic depletion."[43]

Resentment over taxes also exacerbated the racial tensions that had begun to fracture the New Deal Democratic coalition in the 1960s, as discussed in the previous chapter. To some traditional Democratic voters, "not only was the Democratic party aligned with those have-not Americans who belonged to disadvantaged 'groups,' but the party was prepared to impose higher dollar costs on white working men and women in order to advance its commitment to targeted minorities," argues historian Charles Noble. Opposition to welfare spending was particularly strong among white southerners and suburbanites, who "resented federal taxing, spending, and affirmative action policies that were perceived to help inner-city blacks at their expense." As economic conditions worsened, they "simply stopped worrying about the condition of blacks and started thinking about the impact of compulsory, compensatory policies on themselves."[44]

Taxes came to represent "the forcible transfer of hard-earned money away from those who worked to those who did not . . . a forced levy underwriting liberal policies that granted enlarged rights to those members of society who excited the most negative feelings in the minds of other, often angry, voters." In short, conclude the Edsalls, the Democratic Party had "permitted a situation to evolve that encouraged hostility between its taxpaying constituents and non-taxpaying, poor constituents."[45]

The volatile economic and political circumstances of the 1970s opened an opportunity for the newly ascendant representatives of the interests of the business community and the affluent to win approval for a sea change in economic policy . In social critics Frances Fox Piven and Richard Cloward's formulation, the corporate elite launched a "new class war" with the aim of reversing the expansion of the welfare state and "directly redistributing income upward."[46] They argue that the central political implications of popular dissatisfaction with certain social programs, particularly AFDC, as that the conservative right could begin rolling them back "without risking much political opposition."[47]

The end of post-war affluence, coupled with the shock of the first OPEC oil crisis, set in motion a series of convulsions. Historian Michael Katz points out that liberals "lacked a plausible response to the intuitively interconnected problems troubling ordinary Americans: declining opportunity; increased taxes and welfare spending; crime and violence on the streets; and the erosion of family and moral standards." The new public psychology "left Americans receptive to a war on welfare," and conservatives took intellectual as well as political initiative, mounting an argument against the welfare state that attributed to it some measure of responsibility for all of these problems.[48] Rollback of the welfare state became the obvious solution.

Ultimately, however, public opinion did not drive welfare reform efforts. Rather, reform drove public opinion. As historian Stephen Pimpare argues, "Public antipathy to welfare, or, to be more precise, the *perception* of public antipathy to welfare was created . . . [b]y think tanks, foundations, and politicians of both parties with the help of a complicit (if somewhat unknowing) mass media."[49] Like the Victorians of the first Gilded Age, the wealthy elites of the new gilded age adapted a "once discredited discourse in which poverty is a moral failure, aid to the poor itself causes poverty, and government efforts to ameliorate suffering exacerbate it" in order to legitimate and win support for drastic reductions in social welfare spending and the mildly redistributive domestic policies that characterized the liberal welfare state.

Pimpare's arguments are echoed by a range of authors who attribute the rise in popular opposition to the welfare state to a coordinated propaganda campaign mounted by conservative economic, political, and intellectual elites. Books published during the Reagan years, including Charles Murray's *Losing Ground*, Lawrence Mead's *Beyond Entitlement*, and George Gilder's *Wealth and Poverty*, helped broadly disseminate arguments that were once whispered only in the halls of conservative intellectual think tanks. Katz points to "very specific intellectual and political forces" that succeeded in "capitalizing on the dissatisfaction of the working and middle class" to make possible a "fundamental realignment" of economic policy during Reagan's first administration. "A growing body of intellectual justification for both a reduction of domestic social spending and the alteration of the tax system to the distribution advantage of those in the highest income brackets" become a "vital tool of persuasion" for conservative politicians seeking popular support for a major shift in economic policy characterized by cuts to the corporate and capital gains tax rates and the political ascendance of supply-side economics.[50]

Anti-welfare sentiment tapped into resonant, almost archetypal attitudes about poverty and about poor people, about women, about self-sufficiency and the work ethic, and about ethnic or racial stereotypes, and created with them a rationale, a political logic, a philosophical foundation for their preferred policies. Their arguments were then repeated so often in an environment in which alternative arguments were so rare that the public, quite predictably, followed the lead of elites and accepted these arguments as fact. By the mid-1990s, the public debate had shifted so dramatically that even the Democratic Party was willing to do away with the antipoverty apparatus it had constructed during the New Deal and Great Society—or at least its most unpopular parts, namely AFDC, or "welfare." From both Republicans and the Clinton administration, the dominant -message priming attitudes toward welfare reform concerned the evils of the system rather than the welfare of children, and AFDC was left almost devoid of powerful and vocal defenders within the government.

The "remoralization of poverty discourse" in the 1990s led to an increased support in welfare reforms directed toward deterring individuals from obtaining aid, as well as those geared toward reinforcing the work ethic. Both of these principles would become central to the welfare reform legislation enacted in the mid-1990s, which eliminated AFDC in favor of a new program, Temporary Aid to Needy Families (TANF), with its strict time limits.

Thus, the conventional wisdom suggests that the new gilded age, from 1973 through the present, is characterized by ambivalent popular attitudes toward welfare spending that elite discourse manipulated early in the period, drawing on economic and racial tensions in order to ignite a fire of widespread resentment and disapproval for the New Deal/Great Society welfare state. The culmination of that effort, with President Clinton and the Gingrich Congress's successful effort to "end welfare as we know it," highlights the sea change in attitudes toward the social safety net in America.

A different thread of literature challenges this conventional wisdom, arguing instead that basic public attitudes toward the social safety net have remained remarkably stable over time. Many of these studies focus explicitly on public opinion regarding the American welfare state in the mid-1980s, a period when the Reagan administration's retrenchment efforts were in full force. Policy scholars Fay Cook and Edith Barrett polled both the general public and members of the House of Representatives during this period and concluded that "evidence of a true crisis of legitimacy in the American welfare state is sketchy at best."[51] Accounts of the crisis are "anecdotal" and rely on media reports, interpretations of the political success of Ronald Reagan, and conclusions from opinion surveys asking broad, general questions about welfare. Such surveys "often leave the definition of 'welfare' unclear."

On closer examination, Cook and Barrett conclude that public support for the social safety net is "ambiguous," and "the most striking result is how few respondents believe benefits should be decreased for any [welfare] programs; in fact, for no program does a majority of respondents favor decreases." Broad-based programs such as Social Security and Medicare receive greater public support than needs-based programs such as AFDC, but views of AFDC are "not as negative as they are depicted in popular portrayals," and there was no "universal belief that AFDC recipients are undeserving." Indeed, the general consensus reflected support for "federal guarantees of certain social rights, namely the right to medical care, to food, to protection from the risks of unemployment, old age, and sickness."

Based on their analysis of *Los Angeles Times* polling from the mid-1980s, political scientists I. A. Lewis and William Schneider reached similar conclusions, finding "precious little evidence of 'a new selfishness' in American culture."[52] Although the public's "enormous reserve of sympathy for the poor and their plight" was tempered somewhat by its "cynicism and even fatalism about government efforts to eliminate poverty," the public seemed to reject the policy retrenchment embraced by the Reagan administration and other anti-welfare conservatives:

> Americans believe that it is proper and necessary for the federal government to take action to help the poor, even if its record in this area has not been encouraging. . . . People think that a lot of the money we have spent on the poor has been wasted or intercepted; the poor agree. People also acknowledge that we don't really know how to solve the poverty problem; the poor agree with that. But neither of these practical considerations reverses the basic moral consensus that it is a primary responsibility of government to fight poverty.[53]

To that end, the public demonstrated a willingness to pay slightly higher taxes, while large majorities supported government action on behalf of the poor, and agreed with the notion that government ought to spend more rather than less money on poverty programs. Some of the moralism of the elite debate was reflected in popular opinion—such as individual self-reliance, the questionable morality and desert of the poor, and the social and behavioral consequences of welfare dependency—but ultimately Lewis and Schneider conclude from the polling data that the public believes "people are ultimately responsible for their own well-being, but government bears the primary responsibility for helping people when they need it."[54]

Popular attitudes toward the federal government, taxes, and domestic spending from 1973 to 1989 are riddled with complaints that too much tax money is wasted by government. This crankiness "almost disappears" when people were asked what they think government ought to be spending money on. Looking across a range of domestic issues, Americans wanted "more, not less spending," find political scientists Linda and Stephen Bennett. A "basic stability of opinion about federal spending" emerges during the 1970s and 1980s, even amidst the changing political climate and the ascendancy of the conservative right, suggesting that Americans have "a healthy appetite for government spending," one that remained "unsatiated throughout the Reagan era." In short, "Americans demand more from the service state than they are willing to pay for."[55]

Sociologists Lawrence Bobo and Ryan Smith see the same pattern of public opinion: "general stability and almost no sign of abrupt change" and "no indication whatsoever of a general tilt away from commitment to social welfare policies" over the 1973–1991 period. Moreover, "despite discontent with taxes, Americans would support having more of their tax dollars go to support social services."[56] Sociologist Jeffry Will determined that "the American public perceives that poor families with children, in almost all circumstances, are deserving of support and that the level of support needed, and approved, is twice the amount currently provided by government."[57] When respondents were asked to clarify how much was necessary for basic provisions, Will found they held on to the idea of an "income floor below which few . . . believe anyone should fall. . . . [T]his floor is substantially higher than those levels which are covered by current government levels of support."[58]

Taken together, these two strands of the literature—on the one hand, the conventional wisdom regarding the erosion of the support for the welfare state, and on the other, documenting stability in American attitudes toward the role of government in providing a basic social safety net for the poor—seem completely contradictory.

How can they be reconciled? The answer lies in the difference between *specific* programs, particularly AFDC, which was demonized as wasteful, inefficient, and addictive, and the *general* underlying values regarding the social compact between American citizens and the government.

Conventional wisdom focuses heavily on attitudes toward programmatic preferences and opinion regarding "welfare," a term we and others have argued was heavily racialized in the late 1970s and has remained divisive in the decades since. Yet surveys that focus on the broad contours of public attitudes toward the social safety net illustrate remarkable consistency in American support for government intervention to ensure equal opportunity and the provision of a basic floor below which no "deserving" American worker should fall. Americans have always believed in rewarding hard work, and any form of support for the nonworking poor has been politically doomed. "Cash relief" during the Great Depression was meager and limited to specific populations that were not expected to participate in the labor market, especially women and children. The AFDC program of the Great Society was crippled by the racial antagonism of the 1960s, and that animus toward "welfare" persists today.

Indeed, work remains Americans' desired means for helping the poorest Americans. Political scientist Steven Teles concludes, "there is no finding as consistent or as overwhelming in all the survey data I have seen as the support the public gives for guaranteed government jobs programs and other efforts to expand employment."[59] Work is the primary means through which the public desires to help the poor; Americans oppose traditional "welfare" because they believe it violates the work ethic. Political scientist Kent Weaver's examination of public attitudes toward various provisions of Clinton-era welfare reform proposals finds that "the clear public favorite among welfare reform proposals is work requirements, which is consistent with the new paternalism approach to reform."[60] In light of the strong public support for work, the absence of any serious discussion of a public employment program between the New Deal and the Obama administration's 2009 economic recovery package is remarkable.

In the Twilight of the New Gilded Age: Recent Evidence
of Public Support for the Social Safety Net

Little has been written about attitudes toward government's role in providing a social safety net in the decade since the elimination of AFDC and the introduction of TANF in 1994. How do Americans feel now about rising inequality? What level of support do they feel for the government's role in providing a social safety net?

The GSS once again serves as a most useful source of information on this question.[61] Instead of eroding, public support for redistribution actually *increased* somewhat during the 1980s and 1990s. The magnitude of the increase is quite small, but significant across time, suggesting that, unlike their elected Republican leaders, the American public actually was somewhat more receptive to the idea of government redistribution as inequality rose. Specifically, the survey asks, "Do you agree or disagree that it is the responsibility of the government to reduce differences between people with high incomes and low incomes?" In 1987, just 29% either agreed or strongly agreed that government had a responsibility to reduce differences between those with high incomes and those with low incomes, while 47% either disagreed or strongly disagreed with the idea of government reducing income disparities. By 2000, the share agreeing or strongly agreeing that government should reduce income disparities had grown to 34%, while the share disagreeing or strongly disagreeing had shrunk to 41%.

When survey questions turn to specific spending preferences, however, the data suggest far more stability than change. Respondents were asked whether the government spent "too little," "too much," or "about the right amount" of money on a variety of domestic priorities. Domestic spending on "welfare" was generally unpopular, with few (20%) seeing reason to increase government spending. On the other hand, domestic spending on "the poor" was generally viewed as less generous than it should be, with a sizable majority (a pooled average of 63%) answering that the government spends "too little" on the poor. The distinction between "welfare" and "the poor" is clear evidence of the stigma associated with public assistance, as is the dip

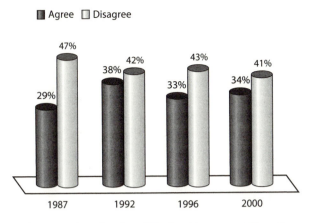

Figure 3.10. Changes in Attitudes about Whether Government Has a Responsibility to Reduce Income Differences between Rich and Poor, 1987–2000
Source: General Social Survey Role of Government Modules I, II, III, and IV

in support for both welfare spending and spending on the poor in the survey immediately following the passage of the welfare reforms of the mid-1990s. We see little change across time, suggesting that the view of the role of government in providing support for the poor remains relatively stable.

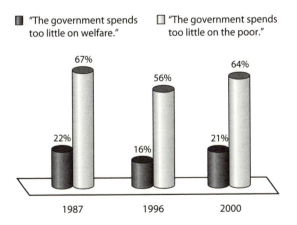

Figure 3.11. Public Preferences for Government Spending: The Distinction between Spending on "Welfare" versus Spending on "the Poor," 1987–2000
Source: General Social Survey Role of Government Modules I, III, and IV

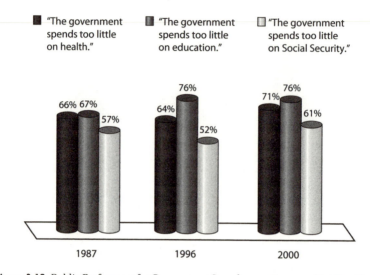

Figure 3.12. Public Preferences for Government Spending on Programs Not Specifically Tied to the Poor, 1987–2000
Source: General Social Survey Role of Government Modules I, III, and IV

Other social programs are more popular and getting more so. The percentage who believe that the government spends "too little" on health increased from 66% in 1987 to over 71% in 2000 and on education spending from 69% to 76% during the same period. Social Security, by now a "sacred" program, was also thought to be underfunded by an increasing majority (from 57% in 1987 to 61% in 2000). When couched in terms of general social spending—rather than specifically targeted to the "poor," or toward "welfare"—the American public is broadly supportive of social safety net spending. Indeed, preferences for social safety net spending have ticked slightly upward in recent years, coinciding with the rise in economic inequality.

The enthusiasm for government spending on education reflects a basic American belief in the role of government in fostering *opportunity*. In keeping with the basic ethos underlying the original ideas behind Johnson's Great Society, Americans offer broad-based support for putting public resources behind programs that seek to equip each individual with a "springboard" for success. In contrast, levels of support for government interventions that reduce the disparity be-

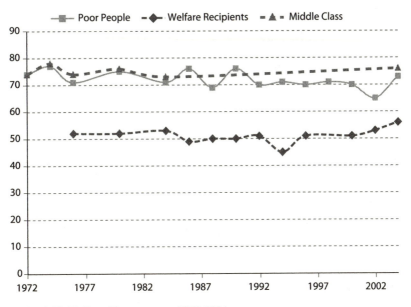

Figure 3.13. Feelings Thermometer, 1972–2004
Note: Average Temperature Range, from 1 ("very cold") to 100 ("very warm"), toward "Welfare Recipients," "Poor People," and "The Middle Class"
Source: National Election Studies

tween rich and poor, that is, those fostering *redistribution*, are far less popular. As figure 3.12 shows, Americans were less convinced that government should step in and reduce income difference between rich and poor over the time period when inequality rose, and the percentage expressing support for redistributive government intervention remained only moderate, at 34%. Once again, the *Economist* magazine's suggestion that Americans want to "join the rich, not soak them" appears to hold. Whether this attitude will persist as evidence of mismanagement on Wall Street grows and Ponzi schemes of immense dimensions explode in the headlines remains to be seen.

These survey questions frame the question in relative terms: "Do you favor *more* spending?" and hence ask the respondents to think about what they prefer compared to the status quo. When we examine preferences for social safety net spending in absolute terms, a remarkable stability is evident over time. This is not the conclusion we would expect if we were to focus our eyes on the election returns over the same time period, for the dominance of conservative politicians who advocated dramatic reduction in social spending is unmistakable. They were moving out ahead of their audience, or perhaps responding to the more extreme elements of it, rather than pursuing policies broadly endorsed.

Did conservatives succeed in bringing their audience along? One way we could approach this question is to ask whether, over the time period of their electoral victories, public attitudes toward the most stigmatized recipients of federal spending changed. The "feelings thermometer" provided by the National Election Studies is useful in this context. It asked respondents to rate their "feelings" toward a variety of groups over the course of the last three decades.

As figure 3.13 illustrates, there is little evidence of change. "Welfare recipients" are viewed with less warmth than are "the poor," suggesting a distinction in respondents' images of the two groups. "The poor," however, are rated surprisingly warmly over time, with thermometer ratings approximately equal to those of the "middle class." Given that the vast majority of Americans consistently state that they are members of the middle class, these thermometer readings suggest a remarkably degree of empathy toward the poor, and an endurance of that empathy across time. If anything, Americans appear to have grown warmer toward the poor and welfare recipients in the early 2000s.

How can we square these incongruous trends? American frustration with economic inequality seems to have grown, and the desire for some form of government intervention seems to have increased accordingly. At the same time, the data display an underlying stability in values with regard to the poor, welfare recipients, and the middle class.

Our answer to this puzzle is simple: the status quo levels of inequality have pushed Americans beyond their comfort zone. Neither underlying preference for equality nor fundamental desires for government intervention have changed dramatically. To the contrary, both remain relatively stable. What has changed is the economic context.

Economic inequalities have grown so severe that many Americans are beyond their breaking point, and are therefore amenable to an increased role for government. The social safety net has become so frayed that many can see the abyss below, and are looking to government for help in reweaving the threads that keep not only the poor but also the middle class from falling through the cracks. The "risk shift" detailed by political scientist Jacob Hacker describes an American safety net where individuals, rather than institutions, are bearing the brunt of major risks—American families bear the burden of providing income, health, and retirement security for themselves, with little help from government or corporations.[62] This shift in risk—a move to what economist Jared Bernstein calls a "you're on your own" framework—has frustrated the American public.[63]

After two decades of sustained economic growth when, in the words of John F. Kennedy, a "rising tide that lift[ed] all boats," the U.S. economy shifted into a fundamentally different mode, characterized by widening inequalities between the rich and poor. While the economic expansions of the 1990s saw a boost for the bottom half of the distribution, the gains at the top far outpaced those at the bottom, and the distance between the rich and the rest stretched ever further. In the economic downturns of the new millennium, income inequality has continued to grow. Median income has remained virtually flat, while incomes at the top spiral higher and higher.

Despite suggestions that part of the explosion in inequality might be attributable to an erosion of social norms around fairness and economic justice in the United States, American public opinion reflects an enduring commitment to a basic modicum of economic fairness. Indeed, tolerance for inequality appears to have decreased as inequality has increased, suggesting that the current record-high levels of inequality are straining Americans' sensibilities regarding the contours of the social compact.

While specific social welfare programs have been the subject of a great deal of controversy over this period of rising economic inequality, underlying attitudes regarding government's role in income redistribution and the provision of a basic social safety net illustrate remarkable stability. If anything, again, the erosion of government's ability to provide for its citizens seems to have stimulated a slight uptick in the desire for spending on social programs, particularly those cast in universalist hues rather than those specifically targeting "the poor."

4 Searching for "the Better Angels of Our Nature"

That's the promise of America, the idea that we are responsible for ourselves, but that we also rise or fall as one nation, the fundamental belief that I am my brother's keeper, I am my sister's keeper. That's the promise we need to keep.

—President Barack Obama

It isn't polls or public opinion of the moment the counts. It is right and wrong leadership that makes epochs in the history of the world.

—President Harry S. Truman

The importance of public opinion in political decision making has been a subject of debate since ancient Greece. Aristotle expressed a deep and abiding faith in the wisdom of crowds, arguing that while the view of any given individual might be suspect, the collective preferences of individuals had special properties of "goodness and intelligence." Plato, on the other hand, foreshadowed Harry Truman's belief in the importance of the measured wisdom of elite leaders, arguing that the public was not to be trusted. To Plato, the crowd was ill-informed, subject to emotional upheaval, and therefore not a sound source of decisions in the public interest.

Policymakers walk the same tightrope today. On the one hand, the work of democracy requires an Aristotelian responsiveness to mass opinion. Not only do elected officials represent the will of those who elected them, but they also are anxious to win reelection and know that unpopular decisions may jeopardize their political futures. On the other hand, policymaking is not a simple call-and-response between voters and their elected officials. In keeping with platonic ideals, political leaders take office with a set of ideals and a bully pulpit, and can use that space to move ahead of their constituents in order to enact bold policies that might seem politically untenable. Politicians play a circular game of follow-the-leader, alternating between following popular opinion and leading in new directions. Today, the interconnection between politics and policymaking—between winning elections and charting the course of the nation—are deeply intertwined. Polling caught on during John F. Kennedy's campaign in 1960 and has remained a mainstay of American politics. Indeed, some of America's best-known political insiders are pollsters—Stan Greenberg and Mark Penn, to name two.

This book has argued that, in the social welfare sphere, presidents have often served as leaders rather than followers. Franklin Roosevelt's New Deal–era social policies were not universally popular, as the polling and archival data presented in chapter one make clear. Indeed, much of the public was concerned about the massive welfare state created by the New Deal policies, and the lines between the deserving and the undeserving were hard and harsh. Similarly, the popularity of Lyndon Johnson's Great Society programs eroded over time, and Richard Nixon's effort to pass the FAP in the early 1970s met a wall of opposition. Yet in the two major eras birthing the foundation of twentieth-century American social welfare policy, presidential administrations often encountered a policy vacuum they could fill, or found themselves farther out on a limb than they had planned, as opposition to their policies gathered force. Each in their own way, Roosevelt, Johnson, and Nixon were mavericks who had to buck public skepticism and the worried advice of their closest advisers.

The suffering of the Great Depression birthed the New Deal, but not without serious dissent from an American public wary of an overly generous welfare state. While millions viewed Roosevelt's policies as a lifeboat, critics did not pull their punches against the administration. From the left, letters poured into the White House decrying the administration's unwillingness to truly take a stand against "Big Business," its failure to implement truly redistributive taxation policies, and its attempts to rein in spending as the price tag of the New Deal began to worry FDR's budget-watchers. From the right, letter writers decried the distribution of cash relief, objected to the provision of the prevailing wage in WPA work sites, and argued vociferously against union rights for public workers. From their perspective, the welfare state simply fed the beast that had created the economic downturn in the first place. It was the absence of the work ethic and old-fashioned initiative that was responsible for growing poverty and joblessness, according to these critics. The New Deal was the first step toward creeping socialism, and that would not do.

The public much preferred public employment and other programs emphasizing work to cash payments or traditional "relief." This emphasis on work echoes throughout the twentieth century, with Americans consistently favoring welfare programs built on the expectation that recipients will be *workers*, not simply recipients of a cash handout. Even so, public workers and others whose work was tied to the state relief system were viewed as second class. An overwhelming majority of the American public believed that WPA workers should be banned from unionizing, and virtually no one believed WPA workers deserved the right to strike. Over three-quarters of the public believed that WPA workers should, as a matter of law, be paid less than similar workers in private industry

While the American worker formed the backbone of those deserving full participation in the welfare state, not all workers were created equal. Immigrants and "vagrants" were excluded from the rolls and viewed with high levels of disdain—residency was a key requirement for full participation, and American notions of belonging hinged on a place-based attachment that neither "aliens" nor those roaming the country in search of better fortunes had earned. Moreover, traditional gender roles excluded women from most benefits provided by the welfare state, as it was built on the firmaments of a worker (i.e., a male) who served as a breadwinner and support for his wife and children. Support for women and children came in the form of mothers' pensions and widows' benefits, but many were excluded altogether—namely, those women who were neither mother nor wife. And, despite popular opinion favoring their inclusion, farmhands and domestic workers were excluded from most New Deal policies as a result of the political coalition carefully crafted by Roosevelt, who relied on southern Democrats favoring the occupational exclusions as a backdoor way of pushing African Americans to the sidelines of the welfare state.

The New Deal era, then, was a period in which the boundaries between deserving and undeserving Americans were underlined, and skepticism (or hostility) over the encroachment of a government-supported welfare state buzzed beneath the surface of policy victories. In some cases, Roosevelt and his team crafted policies that bowed to public opinion, as in the heavy emphasis on work in both the public relief programs and the development of pension policy. But he didn't always follow the dictates of public attitudes, as we learned when we examined opinion polls on occupational exclusions to Social Security. FDR moved to placate his southern congressional opponents at the cost of injecting race-based occupational restrictions into Social Security, even though public opinion did not support these constraints.

Roosevelt was a hero, though, for he followed his convictions in providing an enormous stream of federal funds at a time when powerful interests and plenty of citizens questioned the wisdom of a safety net. By reworking the relationship between government and the economy, Roosevelt stood up not only for the indigent and the unemployed but for an activist conception of the state itself.

The New Deal grew out of the depths of the Great Depression; its encore was molded from the clay of prosperity. In the glory days of the post-war era, poverty was a blight on the American conscience. In a time of plenty, most American agreed with the basic premise behind Lyndon B. Johnson's call to "replace despair with opportunity." Johnson's key weapons in the War on Poverty were human capital–building policies, including Head Start and employment-readiness programs. The war would be won by giving each individual the tools needed to succeed in the booming economy: education and skills. These programs remained popular throughout the period, even as other elements of the Great Society eroded in popularity as racial tensions came to a head.

What remained fundamentally unpopular was any form of hand-out; thus, cash relief viewed as divorced from work was viewed with high levels of suspicion. As early as the mid-1960s, the level of frustration with the perceived lack of effort on the part of the poor was growing. The American public was increasingly likely to view poverty as a result of individual lack of effort rather than as a result of circumstance. While the evolution of American's attitudes toward cash relief is inextricably tied up with the changing racial demographics of America's cities at the time, the underlying message is clear: those who work are deserving of America's generosity, those who don't are not. Johnson rose above popular opinion, enacting Medicaid to provide health care for the poor, including those who were out of the labor force.

The program was not embraced. A strong majority endorsed a government role in medical care to the aged, but many saw little need for care for anyone else except the very poorest of the poor. The mechanism of delivery was just as controversial. By 1965, when Johnson was putting his final touches on his Medicare legislation, over half the country supported a private system in which individuals would simply purchase old-age insurance through private carriers. Medicare, which created a system of health insurance managed by the federal government and funded by an increase in Social Security taxes on working-age individuals, was not the overwhelming people's choice.

While Johnson's achievements via the Great Society have been the topic of praise, criticism, and public debate in the decades since, Nixon's domestic policy efforts have received far less attention. Yet Nixon too was a maverick for his time, a full participant in what sociologist Brian Steensland has called the "failed welfare revolution."[1] With his FAP program, Nixon aimed to provide a minimum income floor for all Americans. The concept of a "guaranteed income" emerged from the halls of academia in the 1960s, and Nixon's efforts to embrace it reflect a quixotic blend of, on the one hand, radical liberalism, and on the other, traditional conservatism. The idea of providing every American with a basic income stipend was far more progressive, in some ways, than the New Deal or Great Society programs that preceded it. A guaranteed income would simply put cash in the hands of families, without strict requirements aimed at coercing behavior or reshaping culture.

In other ways, however, the guaranteed income idea spoke to basic, conservative American ideals. First and foremost, the guaranteed income program was grounded in a laissez-faire economics, with a hands-off approach to the labor market. Within the basic framework of the cash stipend was the assumption that the labor market would perennially produce "losers," poverty was inevitable, and government should not play a major role in improving individuals' labor market opportunities with skills or training. Unlike the New Deal and Great Society programs, which included explicit workforce development components aimed at mitigating poverty by creating opportunity, the FAP focused on economic security by placing a financial floor underneath the poor, working or not, with no complementary training or skills policies. Second, Nixon worked hard to tie the FAP to the idea of work: families who worked but remained poor would receive a boost of support. By consistently using the language of "workfare" over "welfare," Nixon's policies were meant to communicate to a nation frustrated with "lazy" recipients of Great Society largess that his policy rewarded those who played by the rules and worked hard.

The guaranteed income concept was a flop with the American public. In poll after poll, the public rejected the idea of guaranteeing an income floor to American families, and Nixon was unable to effectively connect the dots between work and welfare in order to win over the American people. Nixon's FAP fizzled in the Senate, as liberals fought for a higher minimum income floor and less strict work requirements while conservatives fought the concept of any form of a minimum income.

The legacy of Nixon's ideas lives on, however, in the form of the Earned Income Tax Credit, which Congress enacted with a substantial majority vote during Nixon's last years in office. The EITC, which is essentially the negative income tax that was at the heart of the FAP, provides a tax refund to working poor families. Introduced as a competing policy idea in the waning days of the debate over FAP, the passage of the EITC reflects the high degree of stigma attached to any form of welfare. Elements virtually identical to the EITC existed in the FAP legislation, but the link between welfare and the FAP was too tight to secure any popular support. By severing the tie between welfare and work supports, the EITC was a far more palatable policy for both conservatives and the American public.[2] It has grown over the years into one of the most important poverty-alleviation programs for today's working poor families.

Progressives today often reminisce about the generosity of public spirit that allowed Roosevelt to hammer out the New Deal, and the openness of heart that allowed Johnson to build the Great Society. (Few remember Nixon's domestic policy achievements, and liberals are not often found waxing nostalgic over his administration's accomplishments, thanks to the Watergate debacle.) Yet our examination of mass opinion via public opinion polls and correspondence with the White Houses of both FDR and LBJ suggests quite a different story. A key thread that weaves its way between all three of these eras of social welfare policy development—the New Deal, the Great Society, and even the rise and fall of FAP—is the willingness of elites to reach beyond the boundaries of what the public opinion polls indicate Americans are prepared to accept.

As political scientist John Zaller has noted, elites often follow their own preferences rather than hewing tightly to the preferences expressed by the general public; in this sense, FDR, Johnson, Nixon, and George W. Bush were not unusual in forging policies that diverged from the preferences expressed by the general public.[3] What emerges as surprising is the persistent rejection of the "brother's keeper" approach to government largesse, despite a degree of collective nostalgia to the contrary. While elements of Roosevelt's New Deal were greeted with warmth and enthusiasm, others raised ire. Similarly, while elements of Johnson's Great Society and War on Poverty were cheered at first, others, including the critical development of Medicare, were greeted with ambivalence. Yet both administrations pushed forward, creating a web of social policies that touched on basic points of agreement in society—the deserving poor were those who worked, for instance—but often reached beyond what the polls suggested the median voter embraced.

The precise timing of the polls and letters presented throughout this account vary. Some reflect opinions prior to the implementation of a pathbreaking policy, while others were taken in the aftermath of a major policy's rollout. The consistent message throughout, regardless of whether the poll (or letter) was taken (or written) before or after a policy was implemented, is a limited tolerance for broadly expansive social welfare programs. The story that emerges from this evidence is that American attitudes spring from what political scientist James Stimson calls a "policy mood."[4] Stimson suggests that public opinion acts like a thermostat: when government policy is too liberal for citizens, public opinion demands more conservative policies. The public's embrace of spending cuts in the midst of the New Deal and its hostility to expanded public spending on health insurance in the throes of the Great Society are thus strong indicators that political leaders of the times had gotten out ahead of what the public was willing to accept. Extending the thermostat analogy, the data suggest that political leaders had turned up the heat too high for the general public.

V. O. Key's concept of "latent opinion" provides a second useful framework for understanding the give and take between political elites and public opinion. Key, whose work laid the groundwork for decades of research in American politics and political values, defined "latent opinion" as public opinion that might exist at some future point in response to a decision maker's action and may therefore result in political damage at the polls.[5] As Zaller notes, Key's concept of latent opinion "is not about politicians' *perception* of public opinion" but rather about the "*actual propensities* of public opinion that politicians are prudent to heed."[6] Latent opinion can serve as a powerful constraint on political elites' actions, as politicians may temper their actions avoid offending the public at some point in the future. For instance, Roosevelt may have gotten out ahead of what the public could stomach—in other words, he misread latent opinion—and pulled back on relief efforts in 1937 as an effort to recalibrate his image to better fit the public's desires.

Underlying both Key's and Stimson's argument is a second basic assumption regarding the nature of public opinion that we view the evidence presented in preceding chapters as supporting as well: the general public holds a core of stable preferences, and it does not favor the conventional brother's keeper formula. Across near three-quarters of a century's worth of polls and letters we see limited enthusiasm for public beneficence.[7]

How exactly these administrations were able to usher such controversial programs through Congress and into law is a subject deserving a volume of its own, but a few basic theories provide a starting place. First and foremost, Roosevelt and Johnson both proved to be masters of coalition building. Roosevelt pitted North against South, making a variety of compromises in the legislation (including the ultimate de facto exclusion of African Americans from the New Deal's benefits) in order to secure the passage of the New Deal. Robert Caro's biography of Lyndon Johnson's years in the Senate was titled *Master of the Senate* as a nod to Johnson's impressive negotiating skills, a key element of his success.[8] Johnson brought those skills of negotiation and coalition building to bear on his presidency, and in turn was a "visionary progressive." The failure of the FAP in many ways represented Nixon's failure to master Congress, as the Senate coalition behind the FAP fractured and a new united front of liberals and conservatives mustered the troops to defeat the policy.

Second, both Roosevelt and Johnson benefited from extraordinary times. Roosevelt won office at a time of terrible hardship, and people were desperate for something new. As political scientists Christopher Achen and Larry Bartels have convincingly shown, FDR took office in a year when the main message seemed to be "throw the bastards out."[9] Across the globe, countries enduring economic hardship ushered in new administrations, while those with economic recoveries returned their existing leaders to office. Neither those who were ejected nor those who retained power exhibited any sort of ideological consistency. Economic hardship ushered in administrations of all stripes: conservative, liberal, reactionary, and fascist leadership. On this theory, Roosevelt's electoral success was due more to his promise of something new and the fact that its implementation coincided with an economic upturn (albeit one that didn't end the Depression) rather than with a leftward shift in public opinion. The opposite is true for Lyndon Johnson, who took office at a time of unprecedented economic prosperity. Johnson leveraged this into progressive welfare policy, couching much of his Great Society in terms of creating opportunity in a society that was turning away from its divided, racist past and refashioning itself into one where all Americans, black or white, could have an equal chance.

Third, while Roosevelt, Johnson, and Nixon were "out in front," they made efforts to package or promote their policies in ways that resonated with what was culturally acceptable to the American people. For all three, these accommodations revolved around a pronounced emphasis on the importance of work. The WPA aimed to get needy Americans into jobs in an effort to keep the work ethic from flickering out in a time of slack labor markets. Even though cash relief was cheaper to administer, Roosevelt limited the dole and made it available largely to those who were exempted from the labor market—women and children—rather than able-bodied male workers. The Townsend Plan, a simple and straightforward federal pension, flopped, and hence proposals for Social Security were anchored instead in a citizen's employment history.

Johnson's War on Poverty avoided the promise of cold hard cash to individuals in favor of an emphasis on training that would coax nonworking Americans into the labor market. Further, Johnson's Great Society was couched in a different language from that of the 1930s. Roosevelt's promises of "economic security" were replaced by the language of "opportunity" for economic success. Johnson's Great Society programs aimed to provide a springboard for every American that would allow them to achieve great heights—through education and training—but spoke little about the need for a basic level of economic security.[10]

When President Clinton succeeded in fulfilling his promise to "end welfare as we know it," he benefited from many of the same strategies utilized by Johnson and Roosevelt before him in their successful efforts to reform the welfare state. Like Roosevelt and Johnson, Clinton managed Congress well—a particularly impressive feat, given the divided government over which he presided. Like Roosevelt and Johnson, Clinton couched his reforms in terms that resonated with the American people, with a heavy emphasis on work and individual responsibility. Like Roosevelt and Johnson, Clinton took advantage of the dissatisfaction with the status quo; polls taken in the mid-1990s suggested that Americans preferred virtually any reform to the status quo AFDC program that the TANF program replaced. Clinton's reforms spoke directly to Americans' continued lack of patience for policies that they believed offered "something for nothing," or, in the case of AFDC, cash handouts with little asked of recipients. By requiring able-bodied welfare recipients to participate in some form of job training, Clinton borrowed a page from the successes of the EITC and attempted to link relief to work. A key goal of the reform, the administration argued, was to "make work pay."

Unlike Roosevelt's or Johnson's programs, however, the Personal Responsibility Work Opportunity Reconciliation Act (PRWORA) shrank the welfare state. Time limits and the exclusion of immigrants were reforms that resonated in the polls. Indeed, many have argued Clinton had little leverage to eliminate them, owing to the conservative Republican Congress he faced. Borrowing a page from Nixon's conservative welfare advisers, Clinton couched his reforms in the language of "individual responsibility" and, critics say, offered little in the way of programs aimed at addressing persistent structural barriers to opportunity.[11] Unlike the Great Society's War on Poverty, which aimed to eliminate poverty by providing avenues of opportunity via job training, youth development, and leadership training, Clinton-era welfare reform focused on pushing previously "dependent" welfare recipients into work. The booming economic growth in the second half of the 1990s translated into a reduction in poverty, as well as a reduction in the welfare rolls. Yet the lack of transformative change and the cost of a limited investment in job training have gradually become clear in the 2000s, as the busting of the tech bubble and the economic contraction under the Bush administration pushed 5.7 million individuals back into poverty.[12]

In the years since welfare reform, public opinion on welfare, never a particularly popular program, has remained relatively stable and somewhat more positive than its temporary nadir during the height of the public drama over systemic reform in the mid-1990s. What has changed remarkably during the contemporary period is attitudes toward *inequality*. In precisely the period during which inequality has grown, Americans' tolerance for the level of inequality they are experiencing has dropped. This sea change in opinion is not, however, due to some sort of great awakening on the part of the American public. We did not wake up a nation of wannabe Nordics demanding mass economic equality and redistribution. Americans are still Americans, with a much higher tolerance for economic inequality than our counterparts in other Western postindustrial democracies. What has changed is the landscape around us. The spoils of economic growth are more unequally distributed than ever before, and Americans have reached a tipping point. The United States today is too unequal for most to tolerate, and the polls illustrate this point.

Record-high economic inequality is not the only stressor triggering Americans' collective migraine. Two other key sets of concerns suggest that our national economic headache has multiple causes, all of which are likely working together to create a great deal of anxiety and pain. First, Americans are less sure of their economic footing today than in the past. Economic insecurity has trickled down the socioeconomic ladder to affect not only the blue-collar workers, who have long worried about their ability to continue to stay afloat on rapidly shifting economic seas, but also college-educated white-collar workers, who believed that their educational investment was a solid life jacket for times of economic turbulence. The pace of the development of the global labor market means that even the most highly educated Americans face the prospect of job displacement, and the educational life jacket is looking less and less useful in the face of a tsunami of economic change.

Recent polling data provide ample evidence of American's economic anxiety. For example, a nationally-representative survey jointly sponsored by the Rockefeller Foundation and *Time* magazine found that 72% of Americans feel less financially secure today than they did five years ago. Sixty-six percent say they are not saving enough for retirement, and 23% report experiencing a period with no health insurance coverage in the past year. Of the 2,000 Americans surveyed,

78% agreed that the social contract "has been broken and should be rewritten."[13]

In the shadow of deindustrialization and global competition from nations with inexpensive labor and manufacturing capacity, America's blue-collar workers have long expressed deep concern over their economic prospects. Yet the expanding reach of the global marketplace, combined with a fraying government safety net, has affected a growing share of the labor market, and even those in the "winner's circle" express a creeping sense of malaise. Consumer confidence among college-educated workers and management has plummeted in recent years. White-collar workers are increasingly likely to report financial difficulties, and are far more likely today than in the past to report that they are "likely" to lose their job.

Second, the public is deeply worried that upward mobility is no longer possible for the American family. Individuals worry about their own ability to climb the economic ladder in order to achieve and sustain economic security for their families. Perhaps even more important, parents are no longer confident their children will be able to match their standard of living, much less exceed it. As parents face rising income volatility, eroding wealth (especially in the face of the recent crisis in the mortgage market and ensuing loss in home values), and rising educational costs, their ability to underwrite the upward mobility of the next generation is compromised. In exit polls following the mid-term elections in the fall of 2006, less than one-third of those surveyed said that they thought life would be better for the next generation.[14]

On both of these counts—rising feelings of economic insecurity and rising doubts about the prospect of economic mobility in America—Americans are not simply a "nation of whiners," as Senator McCain's chief economic advisor Phil Graham chided during the 2008 presidential campaign. Compelling evidence on both fronts suggests that Americans are taking a clear-eyed look at the economic reality and expressing justifiable concern.

Family income is less stable today than it was in the early 1970s, with the 1980s and the early 2000s standing out as particularly volatile periods for many. The risk of a large drop in family income has increased markedly for families headed by a college graduate; hence rising anxiety among well-educated workers—those who were supposed to be insured against insecurity by diligent investment in human capital—is well-founded.[15] By 2001, job loss among the college-educated was at a twenty-year high of 11%.[16] Reemployment for all Americans following the loss of a job has become increasingly more difficult, while the unemployment rate for college-educated workers has skyrocketed in the last seven years, increasing by over 40%.[17] *Rates* of unemployment and economic instability remain far lower for college graduates than for those with less education, but the trajectory looks bad because the increase in the risks these families face is more acute.[18] They are not imagining problems; the problems are real enough.

Parents are right to be concerned about their children's prospects for upward economic mobility. The Economic Mobility Project, a partnership sponsored by the Pew Foundation, has found that upward mobility in the United States is far less prevalent than the American dream suggests. Moreover, mobility in the United States has trended *downward* since the 1970s, as America has become a "stickier" society: the poor are more likely to remain poor today, while those born rich are more likely to stay that way. The Pew Report concludes: "In sum, the inequalities of income and wealth have clearly increased, but the opportunity to win the larger prizes being generated by today's economy have not risen in tandem, and, if anything, have declined."[19]

For many, inequality is, by itself, of little concern. America is all about equality of opportunity for upward mobility, not about equality of outcomes. Yet the picture of a highly unequal America with low levels of upward mobility is a very different once from the "city on a hill" image that has propelled America forward as a global beacon of hope for centuries. Limited upward mobility is all the more problematic in a highly unequal society. Upward mobility feels (and indeed can be) far more challenging in a highly unequal society, and Americans have absorbed that lesson uneasily.

Meanwhile, the potential consequences of slipping down the economic ladder have grown more serious. In a slack labor market, finding a new job can be challenging, and the loss of health insurance, pension benefits, and other forms of social insurance that come with it do not make the problem any easier. A college-educated worker displaced from a job in 2001 lost about 23% of his or her earnings.[20] Seventy percent of Americans receive health insurance through an employer-sponsored plan, and the cost of purchasing insurance outside of a group pool is prohibitive.[21] For the millions of workers too well-off to qualify for means-tested Medicaid but too strapped for cash to pay for an individual health care plan, the loss of a job may mean that they are one illness away from financial crisis.

When mature adults experience a downward bump, their children may feel the pain, because parents can no longer support their college expenses. It may be necessary for the next generation to work more hours to make up for the loss of family income. The platform under the next generation wobbles when parents lose their jobs, and this has long-term consequences for intergenerational trajectories.

In a highly unequal society, moving down the economic ladder can mean more social distance between one's peers. Decades of ethnographic research focusing on the inner lives of downwardly mobile families suggest deep feelings of alienation and social dislocation among individual job losers and their families.[22] As economist Robert Frank has suggested, rising inequality creates further social distance between the rich and poor, which has the potential to exacerbate the already painful sociological consequences of downward mobility.[23]

Finally, high levels of inequality and insecurity create resistance to other forms of economic change that can have positive externalities in the long run. As political scientist Kenneth Scheve and economist Matthew Slaughter have compellingly argued, rising inequality has coincided with a surge in protectionist attitudes among the American people.[24] Public support for engagement with the global economy is strongly correlated with labor-market performance, and, for most workers, labor-market performance has been quite poor. Scheve and Slaughter argue that globalization has compelling benefits, with great potential to lift *all* Americans' incomes via enhanced economic performance. Yet globalization in the contemporary era is linked—at least in the public's mind, if not in the minds of economists—to vastly unjust outcomes. While the yachts have been buoyed by a tide of globalization, those in the rowboats and dinghies are drowning. If the United States is to remain a vibrant participant in the world economy, redistributive social policies are an imperative. They cushion the shocks that globalization produces.

In no uncertain terms, the United States is at a major crossroads. The global economy has changed dramatically in the years since Lyndon Johnson inaugurated the building blocks of our contemporary welfare system, to be sure. Government responses to the consequences of economic change over the last eight years have been largely based on antiquated supply-side theories of economics that remain in vogue among only a handful of conservative economists—create economic growth via tax cuts to the rich, and allow the spoils to trickle down to the poor. The result of limited government action in response to the new economy has been its own set of consequences, reinforcing inequality and doing little to create new opportunity in American society.

A wide variety of basic economic indicators color the 2000s as a new gilded age, a period in which the wealthy benefited from government action while working Americans saw little progress. Indeed, in many instances, the average American family lost ground. During the most recent economic expansion, the median income decreased for the first time since the 1920s, while poverty increased. The Bush administration's tax cuts of 2001 provided a windfall to the wealthiest Americans but did little for those in the middle class. According to an analysis by the nonpartisan Tax Policy Center, if the tax cuts are fully phased into law in 2010, the middle fifth of American households will receive an after-tax income boost of just 2.6%, compared to a 5.4% gain for those in the top quintile. The tax cuts have come at a time of skyrocketing federal deficits, as cuts in taxes were not matched by cuts in spending. To the contrary, government spending has skyrocketed to support a protracted and expensive war.

Weak government has had other major consequences as well. Harvard economist and chair of the National Economic Council Lawrence Summers argues that laissez-faire attitudes toward regulation played a significant role in the implosion of the housing and credit markets.[25] Crumbling infrastructure due to limited availability of funds and a hands-off attitude by government surely contributed to the August 2007 collapse of Minneapolis's I-35W bridge, which killed thirteen and injured hundreds. A basic hands-off approach to governing contributed to the Katrina catastrophe, where more than 1,800 people died and the consequences of decades of racism and neglect were laid bare for the nation to watch helplessly on television. Moreover, had government played a more active role in maintaining infrastructure prior to the hurricane, the consequences of Katrina would have been far less dire.

In short, the consequences of nearly a decade of limited government and mismanagement are strikingly clear today. This, no doubt, plays a powerful role in explaining why, despite persistent election victories for conservatives in the 1980s and much of this decade, we also see increasing public support for government intervention on behalf of the nation's working families.

Nbsp;

President Obama faces a set of challenges more daunting than perhaps any since Roosevelt's—a crumbling national economy, a complicated multi-front war, rising global economic challenges, a dysfunctional health care system, and a record low level of trust in government. Yet history tells us that leaders can seize extraordinary opportunities in times of crisis. The limits of the brother's keeper mentality are persistent, and policymakers' efforts to stretch these limits have consistently resulted in backlash, in the form of declining popularity of their ideas.[26] Yet two of the most substantial building blocks of the American social welfare state, the New Deal and the Great Society, occurred at least in part because presidents were willing to step out in front of history early in their tenure. The lesson to

President Obama here is, perhaps, to move quickly and decisively to enact his most ambitious plans as early in his tenure as possible.

Leaders can rise to such a challenge if they recognize that their predecessors have crafted transformative, aggressive change even in the face of resistance from the voting public. In an era of highly sophisticated polling techniques, the pressure to hew closely to "what the people want" can be immense for a politician. President Clinton knew this, and tossed out his forward-looking set of advisers in the mid-1990s in favor of a team that promised to read the polls carefully and help him "triangulate" toward success. Yet both Roosevelt and Johnson—and even Nixon, to a certain extent—worked with public opinion somewhat differently. In creating the building blocks of the progressive welfare state, these leaders paid heed to the polls in order to find useful frames for their messages, and couched their reforms in language that appealed to the public. Yet their concrete policies often moved well beyond what the public felt comfortable with, and they paid little political price for such boldness.

Notes

Introduction

1. Michael Tomasky, "Party in Search of a Notion," *The American Prospect*, May 2006 (www.prospect.org/web/printfriendly-view.ww?id=11424).

2. Here we echo political scientist Martin Gilens, whose book, *Why Americans Hate Welfare: Race, Media, and the Politics of Antipoverty Policy* (Chicago: University of Chicago Press, 2000), first explored the consequences of the racialization of poverty in the public imagination. In that book, Gilens finds that as the image of the poor got blacker, willingness to support expenditures for the poor fell through the floorboards.

3. On this point, see Linda Gordon, *Pitied But Not Entitled: Single Mothers and the History of Welfare* (Cambridge, MA: Harvard University Press, 1998), and Jill Quadagno, *The Color of Welfare: How Racism Undermined the War on Poverty* (New York: Oxford University Press, 1996).

4. See Katherine S. Newman, *Falling From Grace: Downward Mobility in an Age of Affluence* (Berkeley and Los Angeles: University of California Press, 1999).

5. Interviewers relied on quota-controlled polling techniques, which required the researcher to "interview predetermined proportions of people from particular segments of the population," stratifying the sample into a number of exclusive groups that were "thought to capture politically relevant divisions (such as gender and region)." When interviewers actually went out to fill all those cells, the precision of the matches slipped in ways that polling organizations could not control. Most problematic, people "who did not wish to be interviewed were simply replaced with more willing

citizens." These practices introduced distortions that render the enormous body of public opinion material (more than 450 polls conducted before 1950) difficult to use without elaborate weighting schemes. See Adam Berinsky, "American Public Opinion in the 1930s and 1940s: The Analysis of Quota-Controlled Sample Survey Data," *Public Opinion Quarterly* 70, no. 4 (2006): 499.

6. As described in the previous note, the central problem with quota-controlled sample survey data is that many survey samples do not represent certain groups in proportion to their share in the population. As political scientist Adam Berinsky notes, the mismatch between the demographic characteristics of poll samples and the demographics of the population as measured by the census could lead to a mismatch between the views expressed in the polls and those that might have been expressed by the population at large. Berinsky has introduced a straightforward technique for correcting the quota-controlled sample surveys so that they may be viewed as representative of the population at large. He found that the data collected by Gallup and other organizations exhibited a remarkably predictable deviation between the characteristics of the sample and the characteristics of the population.

Using this fact as a starting point, Berinsky constructed a post-stratification weighting scheme. In simple terms, his approach treats the nonrepresentativeness of the quota-controlled sampling procedures as a unit nonresponse problem: certain classes of individuals were either deliberately or inadvertently underrepresented in the samples. Because we have only limited information about the population relative to the sample—auxiliary information from the U.S. Census—the most appropriate correction is a weighting adjustment. Weighting adjustments are typically used to reduce nonresponse bias in survey estimates, and Berinsky's technique applies this lens to the representativeness problem created by quota samples. Berinsky's weights utilize a cell-weighting technique that brings sample proportions in line with the census estimates of the population proportions.

The sample is stratified into a number of cells (J), based on the characteristics of the population deemed important (the matrix of X variables). If the distribution of demographic variables in the sample differs from the distribution in the population, cell weights are used to combine the separate cell estimates into a population estimate by giving extra weight to groups underrepresented in the sample and less weight to overrepresented groups. The remaining question is which demographic characteristics on which to weight. Berinsky argues compellingly that simply using the observable characteristics of respondents to reweight the data is the most parsimonious and reasonable path, and he lays out a hierarchy of desirable observables on which to weight. Education tops this hierarchy, not only because it was a powerful predictor of whom pollsters viewed as "desirable" interview subjects but also because it has an impact on politically relevant variables, was not used as a quota control, and was often measured by survey organizations. In the absence of information on respondents' education, occupation serves as a reasonable proxy. Berinsky has created such weights with great success, making use of the population data in the 1940 census from the Integrated Public Use Microdata Series. We borrow his technique here whenever the data allow for it in order to provide a more reliable picture of New Deal–era public opinion. It is worth noting here that, flaws and all, Gallup's New Deal surveys represented a pioneering step in public opinion research.

7. For more material of this kind, see Robert G. McElvaine, ed., *Down and Out in the Great Depression: Letters from the Forgotten Man* (Chapel Hill: University of North Carolina Press, 1983).

8. Other radio figures, like the populist Father Coughlin or the larger-than-life governor of Louisiana, Huey Long, also received voluminous correspondence, which is discussed at length in Alan Brinkley's authoritative study of populist culture in the 1930s, *Voices of Protest: Huey Long, Father Coughlin, and the Great Depression* (New York: Vintage Books, 1983).

9. As historian Sarah Igo notes, George Gallup and Elmo Roper were the first survey researchers whose ambition was to capture what the national public, the "mass mind," was thinking. Prior to their 1930s polls, survey research focused on distinct subsets of the population, with most attention paid to special groups—criminals, "deviants," the mentally ill, and so forth. Igo's critique of the business of public opinion polling focuses on the homogenization of the population that the creation of a "national average" encouraged. Yet Igo's critique itself provides a solid reason for using public opinion polls as a lens for understanding national attitudes toward social welfare. As she notes, beginning in the New Deal and continuing through the present day, public opinion surveys have played a critical role for those seeking to understand the mood of the general public. While national

aggregate statistics may indeed mask layers upon layers of diverse opinions among various groups, the "mass mind" has long been an important indicator for understanding America. Political scientists, sociologists, and political and marketing gurus have long used aggregate statistics as a basic tool for making sense of the world, and we build on that tradition in this book. While disaggregating by race, region, party, or other demographic categories of interest would certainly be a useful enterprise, our aim in this book is to provide an overview capturing the national mood, not an exhaustive survey charting the many contours of public attitudes across the century. See Sarah E. Igo, *The Averaged American: Surveys, Citizens, and the Making of a Mass Public* (Cambridge, MA: Harvard University Press, 2007).

10. Two of Johnson's most important initiatives, Medicare and Medicaid, were redistributive in effect if not in intention because they provided services to the elderly and the poor who would otherwise have had to spend real dollars on health care. Ironically, Medicaid was added to the agenda in an effort to make it more difficult to extend Medicare into a genuinely national insurance system. John B. Williamson and Diane M. Watts-Roy, "Framing the Generational Equity Debate," in Williamson et al., *The Generational Equity Debate* (New York: Columbia University Press, 1999), 10.

CHAPTER 1

1. Various reports reprinted in memo titled "Work Relief Comment," no sender or recipient information, March 5, 1935, Box 68, Papers of Harry L. Hopkins, Franklin D. Roosevelt Presidential Library and Museum, Hyde Park, NY.

2. Irving Bernstein, *The Lean Years: A History of the American Workers, 1920–1933* (Boston: Houghton Mifflin, 1972), 416.

3. Arthur M. Schlesinger Jr., *The Crisis of the Old Order: 1919–1933, The Age of Roosevelt* (New York: Mariner Books, 2003), 155.

4. Mrs. Carl Brenden to President Roosevelt, May 9, 1934; Box 2, President's Personal File (PPF) 200; Papers of Franklin D. Roosevelt; Franklin D. Roosevelt Presidential Library and Museum, Hyde Park, NY.

5. Lizabeth Cohen, *Making a New Deal: Industrial Workers in Chicago, 1919–1939* (New York: Cambridge University Press, 1991).

6. Robert and Helen Lynd, sociologists studying the hard-hit factory town of Muncie, Indiana, at the time of the Depression, watched as local institutions collapsed under the strain. The Lynds noted that while "charity in Middletown in 1925 was overwhelmingly a private affair, and it was felt to be proper that it remain so," the Depression created demands that local organizations could not cope with. Robert S. Lynd and Helen Merrell Lynd, *Middletown in Transition: A Study in Cultural Conflicts* (New York: Harcourt Brace Jovanovich, 1982 [1937]), 142.

7. Cohen, *Making a New Deal*, 215.

8. See Edwin Amenta, *Bold Relief: Institutional Politics and the Origins of Modern American Social Policy* (Princeton, NJ: Princeton University Press, 1998), and Theda Skocpol, *Protecting Soldiers and Mothers: The Political Origins of Social Policy in the United States* (Cambridge, MA: Belknap Press of Harvard University Press, 1992).

9. Max Baron to President Roosevelt, December 11, 1933, Box 129, PPF 200, Roosevelt Papers; Roosevelt Presidential Library.

10. John Binkley to President Roosevelt, January 1, 1934, Box 129, PPF 200, Roosevelt Papers, Roosevelt Presidential Library.

11. Rovaida T. Murray to President Roosevelt, March 17, 1935, Box 141, PPF 200, Roosevelt Papers, Roosevelt Presidential Library.

12. B. A. Bonte to President Roosevelt, May 8, 1934, Box 2, PPF 200, Roosevelt Papers, Roosevelt Presidential Library.

13. O. Caswell to President Roosevelt, April 18, 1934, Box 2, PPF 200, Roosevelt Papers, Roosevelt Presidential Library.

14. V. Lowell Bronn to President Roosevelt, March 8, 1935, Box 2, PPF 200, Roosevelt Papers, Roosevelt Presidential Library.

15. S.H. Marsh to President Roosevelt, September 29, 1934, Box 141, PPF 200, Roosevelt Papers, Roosevelt Presidential Library.

16. Harry Berg to President Roosevelt, February 17, 1934, Box 2, PPF 200, Roosevelt Papers, Roosevelt Presidential Library.

17. Sentinels of the Republic to President Roosevelt, May 6, 1933, Box 2, PPF 200, Roosevelt Papers, Roosevelt Presidential Library.

18. Kenneth de Vos to President Roosevelt, May 11, 1934, Box 3, PPF 200, Roosevelt Papers, Roosevelt Presidential Library.

19. Charles Stephens to President Roosevelt, April 4, 1935, Box 5, PPF 200, Roosevelt Papers, Roosevelt Presidential Library.

20. Roy Kerr Eldridge to President Roosevelt, June 29, 1935, Box 3, PPF 200, Roosevelt Papers, Roosevelt Library.

21. Burl Cross to President Roosevelt, July 2, 1936, Box 3, PPF 200, Roosevelt Papers, Roosevelt Presidential Library.

22. E. E. Denne to President Roosevelt, November 23, [no year], Box 3, PPF 200, Roosevelt Papers, Roosevelt Presidential Library. Denne's views presage a theme in a much later theme contained in Richard Sennett and Jonathan Cobb's 1970 classic *The Hidden Injuries of Class* (New York: Vintage Books, 1972). Sennett and Cobb discuss the resentment working people felt toward those on welfare on the grounds that the latter were smart enough to game the system, while the taxpaying workers were, in a sense, not clever enough to follow suit. The objection was less on moral grounds and more on the grounds of having been duped.

23. Orrin [last name illegible] to President Roosevelt, August 30, 1934, Box 5, PPF 200, Roosevelt Papers, Roosevelt Presidential Library.

24. Mrs. George Carsey to President Johnson, May 26, 1934, Box 2, PPF 200, Roosevelt Papers, Roosevelt Presidential Library.

25. Irwin Spear to President Roosevelt, February 10, 1936, Box 5, PPF 200, Roosevelt Papers, Roosevelt Presidential Library.

26. John Snyder to President Roosevelt, April 15, 1935, Box 5, PPF 200, Roosevelt Papers, Roosevelt Presidential Library.

27. Michael Katz, *In the Shadow of the Poorhouse: A Social History of Welfare in America* (New York: Basic Books, 1986), 209–11, 223.

28. Ibid.

29. Robert Bremner, "The New Deal and Social Welfare," in *Fifty Years Later: The New Deal Evaluated*, ed. Harvard Sitkoff (New York: Knopf, 1984), 75. E. Wight Bakke, who contributed some of the most enduring portraits of the Depression in his classic book, *The Unemployed Worker*, also notes a softening attitude toward the unemployed as the Depression deepened. E. Wight Bakke, *The Unemployed Worker: A Study of the Task of Making a Living without a Job* (Hamden, CT: Archon Books, 1969 [1940]), 319–21.

30. William Brock, *Welfare, Democracy and the New Deal* (New York: Cambridge University Press, 1988), 166–67.

31. The original data are not in the archives and hence we do not have the demographics of the respondents that would permit us to weight the responses properly.

32. New Deal–era polls often asked respondents for their opinion on "federal relief," which is a vague term that may have meant different things to different respondents. Relief efforts during the New Deal encompassed an array of programs, and we have no good way of knowing what a given respondent was thinking when he or she offered pollsters an opinion on "federal relief spending." Regardless of what the term "relief" meant to a given respondent, however, the polls demonstrate that the general public sentiment was mixed. We view this as evidence of a skepticism of New Deal efforts to extend the government's safety net.

33. Brock, *Welfare, Democracy and the New Deal*, 336, 351.

34. Under clause 7A of the National Industrial Recovery Act, government was responsible for the protection of unions and collective bargaining. Corporations that wanted to be part of the NIRA program had to agree to these provisions and bargain in good faith. The NIRA was later struck down by the Supreme Court, and clause 7A was replaced by the Wagner Act.

35. H. S. Adler to President Roosevelt, August 17, 1934, Box 3, PPF 200, Roosevelt Papers, Roosevelt Presidential Library.

36. From the collection of letters to radio editorialist Boake Carter, *Johnny Q Public Speaks! The Nation Appraises the New Deal* (New York: Dodge Publishing Co., 1936).

37. Robert Bremner captures well the durability of American anti-welfare sentiments:

> Generous sympathy for those known to be in need mingles with fear of being duped and misgivings about the need and consequences of heavy outlays for the unknown and faceless poor. In providing relief and work projects for large numbers of the unemployed, Roosevelt overcame some of the traditional fears and misgivings about public aid, but these reservations acted as a brake on developing more adequate provision of public assistance for all who needed it.

See Bremner, "The New Deal and Social Welfare," 86.

38. William Snider to President Roosevelt, January 10, 1939, Box 5, PPF 200, Roosevelt Papers, Roosevelt Presidential Library.

39. From the collection of letters to radio editorialist Boake Carter, *Johnny Q Public Speaks!*

40. Ibid.

41. Ibid.

42. Contemporary studies of farm foreclosures suggest a similar unforgiving attitude. Kathryn Dudley's research on the loss of family farms in the Midwest in the 1980s makes it clear that neighbors waited to pounce on equipment and land at auction when their overly encumbered friends went bankrupt. Highly moralistic accounts of imprudent spending or poor management skills dominated their explanations of what had befallen their fellow farmers; little was said about aggressive banks urging farmers to take on debt in an earlier, better time. See Kathryn Dudley, *Debt and Dispossession: Farm Loss in America's Heartland* (Chicago: University of Chicago Press, 2002).

43. Willard Davis to President Roosevelt, December 6, 1934, Box 3, PPF 200, Roosevelt Papers, Roosevelt Presidential Library.

44. The stigma attached to relief was as humiliating as it was deliberate. In most localities, relief recipients were required to sign a pauper's oath, declaring themselves absolutely destitute. Relatives had to be asked for support first, and if they refused they could be prosecuted. In most states, relief recipients were stripped of the right to vote or run for office. Relief was delivered not in the form of actual cash but as "in kind" benefits of surplus food, cotton, and clothing from WPA sewing rooms. Only in the late 1930s did emergency relief become a system of cash outlays. As one historian put the matter, "To be 'on the town' or 'on the county' was the lowest state outside prison to which a member of the community could descend." See Josephine Chapin Brown, *Public Relief: 1929–1939* (New York: Holt, Rinehardt and Winston, 1940).

45. There is only one exception to this otherwise ironclad set of findings on cash relief: In response to a January 9, 1938, Gallup survey asking, "Do you think it is the government's responsibility to pay the living expenses of needy people who are out of work?" 69% answered yes and 31% answered no. We are unsure how to interpret this result, since it is at sharp variance with all of the other evidence and because "living expenses" is a difficult term to parse. Moreover, we are unable to weight the data to correct for sampling error, so it should be viewed with appropriate skepticism. Poll reprinted in general office memo, "Summary of Public Opinion Relating to the WPA and Relief," 4, February 20, 1939, Box 55, Hopkins Papers, Roosevelt Library.

46. Ibid, 8. Data from a Gallup Fortune Executive Outlook Survey from October 1936, cited in Hadley Cantril and Mildred Strunk, *Public Opinion, 1935–1946* (Princeton, NJ: Princeton University Press, 1951). We are unable to weight the data to correct for any potential sampling error.

47. As quoted in Cass Sunstein's excellent book on the business left unfinished by Roosevelt's New Deal, *The Second Bill of Rights: FDR's Unfinished Revolution and Why We Need It More Than Ever* (New York: Basic Books, 2004).

48. Holzoff was a staffer on Roosevelt's Committee on Economic Security. See Alexander Holzoff, "Some Popular Misconceptions Regarding Unemployment Compensation" (http://www.ssa.gov/history/reports/ces/ ces1 holtzhoff.html; originally published September 1934).

49. Donald Howard, *The WPA and Federal Relief Policy* (New York: Russell Sage Foundation, 1943), 44, 830–35.

50. The CWA was an early forerunner of the WPA. The CWA put 4.2 million people to work in only three months but was ultimately terminated, owing to political battles that arose because of internal disputes within the Roosevelt administration over whether the government should be involved in the direct provision of jobs to the unemployed.

51. Alvie Atkinson to President Roosevelt, November 23, 1934, Box 127, PPF 200, Roosevelt Papers, Roosevelt Presidential Library.

52. Bakke, *The Unemployed Worker*; Mirra Komarovsky, *The Unemployed Man and His Family: The Effect of Unemployment Upon the Status of the Man in Fifty-Nine Families* (Lanham, MD: AltaMira Press, 2004 [1940]). See also Ruth Cavan and Katherine Ranck, *The Family and the Depression: A Study of One Hundred Chicago Families* (Chicago: University of Chicago Press, 1938), and Robert Angell, *The Family Encounters the Depression* (New York: Scribner's Sons, 1936).

53. Public Health Nurses of the Hygenic Institute to President Roosevelt, December 20, 1933, Box 141, PPF 200, Roosevelt Papers, Roosevelt Presidential Library.

54. Adam [last name illegible] and John Glab to President Roosevelt, November 30, 1933, Box 141, PPF 200, Roosevelt Papers, Roosevelt Presidential Library.

55. Robert [last name illegible] to President Roosevelt, December 11, 1933, Box 129, PPF 200, Roosevelt Papers, Roosevelt Presidential Library.

56. Caleb Moore to President Roosevelt, January 6, 1935, Box 141, PPF 200, Roosevelt Papers, Roosevelt Presidential Library.

57. Rovaida T. Murray to President Roosevelt, March 17, 1935, Box 141, PPF 200, Roosevelt Papers; Roosevelt Presidential Library.

58. Gallup, January 10, 1940, Survey 180-A, Q7b, weighted to correct for sampling error. Their views were endorsed by even the most enthusiastic of New Deal policymakers. The idea of public employee unions was a proposition entertained by fringe radicals, if that, but hardly embraced by the mainstream. The Gallup data are available from the Roper Center for Public Opinion Research, University of Connecticut, Storrs.

59. Gallup, August 6, 1939, Survey 164-A, Q4, weighted to correct for sampling error. The Gallup data are available from the Roper Center for Public Opinion Research, University of Connecticut.

60. Gallup, August 11, 1939, Survey 165-A, Q2. These data are not weighted and represent a very narrow segment of the population. The Gallup data are available from the Roper Center for Public Opinion Research, University of Connecticut, Storrs.

61. See Carter, *Johnny Q Public Speaks!*

62. Bakke pointed out that the "make-work" nature of many of the relief projects that often required low or unskilled work to explain why "relief work is not rated as a 'swell job' by anyone." Bakke, *The Unemployed Worker*, 258–60.

63. Jason Scott Smith, *Building New Deal Liberalism: The Political Economy of Public Works, 1933–1956* (New York: Cambridge University Press, 2005).

64. See Gordon, *Pitied But Not Entitled*, 211, 223–25, 241; and Cohen, *Making a New Deal.*

65. See Viviana A. Zelizer, *The Social Meaning of Money: Pin Money, Paychecks, Poor Relief, and Other Currencies* (Princeton, NJ: Princeton University Press, 1997).

66. 1936 AIPO/Gallup poll, weighted. The Gallup data are available from the Roper Center for Public Opinion Research, University of Connecticut, Storrs.

67. See Edwin Amenta, *When Movements Matter: The Townsend Plan and the Rise of Social Security* (Princeton, NJ: Princeton University Press, 2006).

68. See, e.g., T. H. Watkins, *The Hungry Years: A Narrative History of the Great Depression in America* (New York: Henry Holt, 1999).

69. As noted at www.californiahistory.net/9pages/panaceas_townsend .htm. See also Amenta, *When Movements Matter*.

70. See Amenta, *When Movements Matter*.

71. It probably did not help the cause that Townsend was caught in a major embezzlement scandal.

72. See Amenta, *When Movements Matter*.

73. Roosevelt's staff on the Committee of Economic Security had distinct views on the nature of the program they were at work designing:

> Social insurance is an institution designed to prevent destitution and dependency. Destitution and dependency are enormously expensive, not only in the initial cost of necessary assistance, but in the disastrous psychological effect of relief upon the recipients, which in turn breeds more dependency. . . . The quality of self-respect which perhaps more than any other helps to build and maintain a sturdy community has an important dollar and cent value to society. Government contribution to social insurance is based upon recognition of this situation. It amounts to a dedication to the policy of putting public funds into keeping people out of a state of destitution in substitution for the policy of charitable assistance for them after dependency has become a fact. (Committee on Economic Security Staff, "Old Age Security Staff Report," http://www.ssa.gov/history/reports/ces/ces2armstaff.html, originally published in January 1935).

Theda Skocpol has highlighted the effective "targeting within universalism" accomplished by Social Security, which was highly redistributive while simultaneously embracing all citizens, regardless of income. See Theda Skocpol, "Targeting Within Universalism: Politically Viable Policies to Combat Poverty in the United States," in *The Urban Underclass*, ed. C. Jencks and P. Peterson (Washington, DC: Brookings Institution Press, 1991).

74. The Report to the President of the Committee on Economic Security makes the intentional divergence from the European model of social insurance very clear:

The program for economic security we suggest follows no single pattern. It is broader than social insurance and does not attempt merely to copy European methods. In placing primary emphasis on employment, rather than unemployment compensation, we differ fundamentally from those who see social insurance as an all-sufficient program for economic security. We recommend wide application of the principles of social insurance, but not without deviation from European models. Where other measures seemed more appropriate to our background or present situation, we have not hesitated to recommend them in preference to the European practices. In doing so we have recommended the measures at this time which seemed best calculated under our American conditions to protect individuals in the years immediately ahead from hazards which plunge them into destitution and dependency. This, we believe, is in accord with the method of attaining the definite goal of the Government, social justice, which was outlined in the message of January 4, 1935. We seek it through tested liberal traditions, through processes which retain all of the deep essentials of that republican form of government first given to a troubled world by the United States. (Committee on Economic Security Staff, "Old Age Security Staff Report," January 1935)

75. Williamson and Watts-Roy, "Framing the Generational Equity Debate," 8.

76. It was not helped by the scandals that surrounded it or by the competition from other pension organizations, discussed at length in Amenta, *When Movements Matter*.

77. Gordon, *Pitied But Not Entitled*, 195. See also Alice Kessler-Harris, *In Pursuit of Equity: Women, Men and the Quest for Economic Citizenship in 20th Century America* (New York: Oxford University Press, 2001); Gwendolyn Mink, *The Wages of Motherhood: Inequality in the Welfare State, 1917–1942* (Ithaca, NY: Cornell University Press, 1995); and Chad Alan Goldberg, *Citizens and Paupers: Relief, Rights and Race, from the Freedmen's Bureau to Workfare* (Chicago: University of Chicago Press, 2007).

78. Nonwhites were also more relief friendly than whites, but because there were so few nonwhites in the sample, the results are not statistically significant. Age was not a significant predictor of attitudes toward relief.

79. James Patterson, *America's Struggle against Poverty in the Twentieth Century* (Cambridge, MA: Harvard University Press, 2000), 45.

80. For more on this point, see Bruce Shulman, *From Cotton Belt to Sun Belt: Federal Policy, Economic Development, and the Transformation of the South 1938–1980* (Durham, NC: Duke University Press, 1994).

81. Mrs. J.R.R. McEwen to President Roosevelt, September 15, 1935, Box 4, PPF 200, Roosevelt Papers, Roosevelt Presidential Library.

82. George Davis to President Roosevelt, October 1, 1936, Box 3, PPF 200, Roosevelt Papers, Roosevelt Presidential Library.

83. See Robert C. Lieberman, *Shifting the Color Line: Race and the American Welfare State* (Cambridge, MA: Harvard University Press, 2001).

84. See Ira Katznelson, *When Affirmative Action Was White: An Untold History of Racial Inequality in Twentieth-Century America* (New York: W. W. Norton, 2006), 22.

85. Gilens, *Why Americans Hate Welfare*.

86. Quadagno, *The Color of Welfare*, 19–24.

87. Non-citizens were a suspect category. In 1939—two years before Pearl Harbor and the surge of anti-Japanese sentiment—84% of Americans believed that all persons living in the United States who were not citizens should be "fingerprinted and registered with the federal government." Gallup, January 27, 1939, Survey 144-A, Q5, not weighted.

88. A 1940 poll reported that 95% of Americans agreed that "people who are not United States citizens should have to register with the government." AIPO, June 9, 1940, weighted to correct for sampling error.

89. F. E. Balderrama and R. Rodriguez, *Decade of Betrayal: Mexican Repatriation in the 1930s* (Albuquerque: University of New Mexico Press, 1995).

90. AIPO, December 1935, not weighted. The data are available from the Roper Center for Public Opinion Research, University of Connecticut, Storrs.

91. AIPO, December 1938, weighted to correct for sampling error. The data are available from the Roper Center for Public Opinion Research, University of Connecticut, Storrs.

92. AIPO, January 1939, weighted to correct for sampling error. The data are available from the Roper Center for Public Opinion Research, University of Connecticut, Storrs.

93. Mrs. J Robert Smith to President Roosevelt, August 15, 1938, Box 5, PPF 200, Roosevelt Papers, Roosevelt Presidential Library.

94. Leon Brown to President Roosevelt, October 31, 1934, Box 2, PPF 200, Roosevelt Papers, Roosevelt Presidential Library.

95. Roger Daniels's excellent *Guarding the Golden Door: American Immigration Policy and Immigrants Since 1882* (New York: Hill and Wang, 2004) illustrates the interplay between social welfare policy and immigration policy. Daniels argues that U.S. willingness to admit immigrants was contingent on the immigrants' likelihood of becoming dependent on the public purse. Daniels traces the doctrine to 1882 statutory language intended to limit Chinese immigration, which stated that consular officers could deny entry to "paupers or persons likely to become a public charge." While the original language from the late nineteenth century intended to exclude not poor people generally, only "those who were incapable of supporting themselves," a 1930 extension of this statute went one step further. Daniels quotes a 1930 State Department release: "If the consular officer believes that the applicant [for entry] may probably become a public charge at any time, even during a considerable period subsequent to his arrival, he must refuse the visa" (ibid., 61).

96. From the collection of letters to radio editorialist Boake Carter, *Johnny Q Public Speaks!*

97. Ibid.

98. P. A. Adams to President Roosevelt, November 4, 1935, Box 2, PPF 200, Roosevelt Papers, Roosevelt Presidential Library.

99. The question actually referred both to the respondent's place of work and to his or her spouse's workplace.

100. NORC, May 1942, weighted. The data are available from the Roper Center for Public Opinion Research, University of Connecticut, Storrs.

101. NORC, October 1942, weighted. The data are available from the Roper Center for Public Opinion Research, University of Connecticut, Storrs.

102. For an excellent illustration of this point in the context of welfare policy, see Cybelle Fox, "The Changing Color of Welfare? How Whites' Attitudes toward Latinos Influence Support for Welfare," *American Journal of Sociology* 110, no. 3 (2004): 580.

103. Roger Daniels's account quotes an Indiana man who remembered well what happened. "So they told [them] 'You are making $7 or $8 per payday for your family. You can't feed them, you can't do nothing. So we are going to take you off welfare.' 'Oh God . . . We'll starve!' 'No, no you have an alternative . . . go to Mexico. We have a train . . . full of Mexican people [that] will stop on the corner of Michigan and Guthrie, on the Pennsylvania Railroad. And they will head for Mexico. In Mexico you will transfer, and we'll take you where you come from, close, not actually there, but to the closest town.' So actually they weren't forcing [them] to leave, they gave [them] a choice, starve or go back to Mexico." See Daniels, *Guarding the Golden Door*, 61. See also Cybelle Fox, "Expelling the 'Aliens': The Deportation and Repatriation of Destitute Mexicans and Europeans," presented at the Social Science History Conference, Chicago, November 2007.

104. L. R. Akins to President Roosevelt, June 15, 1934, Box 2, PPF 200, Roosevelt Papers, Roosevelt Presidential Library.

105. Kessler-Harris, *In Pursuit of Equity*; Gordon, *Pitied But Not Entitled*; Mink, *The Wages of Motherhood*; Skocpol, *Protecting Soldiers and Mothers*.

106. Alice Kessler-Harris argues that work anchored nineteenth-century claims to political participation, but when the federal government tied wage work to "tangible, publicly provided rewards, employment emerged as a boundary line demarcating different kinds of citizenship. Casual laborers, the unskilled and untrained, housewives, farm workers, mothers and domestic servants all found themselves on the side of a barrier not of their making. Their own benefits not earned but means-tested, classified as relief, not rights." Here she draws on British social theorist T. H. Marshall's three categories of citizenship—civil, political, and social. The New Deal–era decision to base social citizenship on work was a key organizing principle that defined women as out of the picture. Those women who did work were often in and out of the workforce to the extent that they never qualified for the social insurance components built into the New Deal. See Kessler-Harris, *In Pursuit of Equity*, 4.

107. Ironically, women and children were thought to be appropriate targets for cash relief precisely because the "right to work" was not one that ordinary people wanted to see extended to women, particularly mothers. As

others have argued, mothers were supposed to stay home, both to care for their children and to avoid competing with men for employment. While it is tempting to see this as an element of blind sexism, it should also be remembered that the industries employing predominantly men were the hardest hit by the Depression; to the extent that they remained open, they often did so by shifting to cheaper sources of labor (including women and children). Hard as it was to find work during the darkest days, it was often easier for women to do so than men. Moreover, as factories began to revive, they often sought out female labor, again to keep their costs down. Hence a complicating motivation for making mothers eligible for cash relief was precisely to keep them out of the labor market where their presence had a dampening impact on male employment.

108. After prolonged debate, Kessler-Harris notes, this provision was excluded. The whole idea of full employment was eliminated because the House could not agree on whether the government should guarantee full employment. Ultimately, Truman signed the Full Employment Act of 1946, but it was more a list of suggestions about how to achieve full employment than any kind of guarantee. See Kessler-Harris, *In Pursuit of Equity.*

109. Some scholars (notably Lizabeth Cohen) have argued that college attendance was increasing anyway. Yet even those who caution against overly positive interpretations of the impact of the GI Bill would agree that it accelerated the trend. See Lizabeth Cohen, *A Consumers' Republic: The Politics of Mass Consumption in Postwar America* (New York: Vintage, 2003).

110. The rejection of occupational restrictions on eligibility for Social Security is one of the rare exceptions.

111. For this we need to look to research by Steven Attewell, whose forthcoming doctoral dissertation in the Department of History at the University of California, Santa Barbara, speaks directly to this question.

112. Christopher Achen and Larry Bartels, "Partisan Hearts and Gall Bladders: Retrospection and Realignment in the Wake of the Great Depression," presented at the annual meeting of the Midwest Political Science Association, Chicago, April 7–9, 2007.

113. It is perhaps particularly notable that FDR's margin of victory was narrower during the Second World War, when Americans might have been expected to endorse him even more strongly (not only for nationalist reasons but for the tightening of labor markets that pushed the country closer to

full employment than it had been in a decade). See Matthew A. Baum and Samuel Kernell, "Economic Class and Popular Support for Franklin Roosevelt in War and Peace," *Public Opinion Quarterly* 65 (2001): 198–229.

CHAPTER 2

1. Frances Fox Piven and Richard Cloward have provided a more political analysis of the Office of Economic Opportunity, arguing that the OEO was an attempt by the Democratic Party to work around the city machines and reach directly to the grass roots. Frances Fox Piven and Richard Cloward, *Regulating the Poor: The Functions of Public Welfare* (New York: Vintage, 1971).

2. Michael B. Katz, *The Undeserving Poor: From the War on Poverty to the War on Welfare* (New York: Pantheon, 1989). To be sure, financial constraints were part of the impetus to Johnson's emphasis on education and training. Public employment was much more expensive, and Johnson was under pressure to hold the cost of the War on Poverty down. For more on this issue, see Judith Russell, *Economics, Bureaucracy and Race: How Keynesians Misguided the War on Poverty* (New York: Columbia University Press, 2003).

3. Joshua Freeman, "Tricky Dick's Legacy: A Review of Rick Perlstein's *Nixonland*," *Dissent*, Summer 2008.

4. Clem Brooks and Jeff Manza, *Why Welfare States Persist: The Importance of Public Opinion in Democracies* (Chicago: University of Chicago Press, 2007).

5. Gallup, October 1967 survey (USGALLUP.753.Q23) at the Roper Center for Public Opinion Research, University of Connecticut, Storrs.

6. Theodore Marmor, *The Politics of Medicare* (Chicago: Aldine, 1973), quoted in Williamson et al., *The Generational Equity Debate*, 10.

7. The FAP failed to pass because it incited opposition from two completely different partisan groups: conservatives who hated the whole idea, and liberals who were convinced they could win something even more generous, like the plan suggested by McGovern and championed by welfare rights advocates.

8. John Kenneth Galbraith, *The Affluent Society* (Boston: Houghton Mifflin, 1958); Eugene McCarthy, *A Liberal Answer to the Conservative Challenge*

(Santa Barbara, CA: Praeger, 1965); Michael Harrington, *The Other American: Poverty in the United States* (New York: Macmillan, 1962).

9. The Harlem riot took place in July 1964. It was followed in August 1965 by the massive Watts riot.

10. President Lyndon B. Johnson's Remarks at the University of Michigan, on May 22, 1964. See Lyndon B. Johnson, *Public Papers of the Presidents of the United States: Lyndon B. Johnson, 1963–1964,* vol. 1, 704–7 (Washington, DC: Government Printing Office, 1965).

11. President Lyndon B. Johnson's Remarks Before the National Convention upon Accepting the Nomination, on August 27, 1964. Johnson, *Public Papers of the Presidents of the United States,* 1:1000–13.

12. Russell, *Economics, Bureaucracy and Race.*

13. President Johnson listed the following programs as critical elements of his war on poverty: (1) "special effort" in the chronically depressed areas of Appalachia; (2) expansion of the area redevelopment program; (3) youth employment legislation "to put jobless, aimless, hopeless youngsters to work on useful projects"; (4) distribution of food to the needy via an expanded food stamp program; (5) the creation of a National Service Corps to help the economically deprived of our own country as the Peace Corps helps those abroad; (6) the modernization of unemployment insurance; (7) a "commission on automation," because "if we have the brain power to invent these machines, we have the brain power to make certain they are a boon and not a bane to humanity"; (8) extended coverage of workers by the minimum wage law; (9) special school aid funds to improve the quality of teaching, training, and counseling in "our hardest hit areas"; (10) the construction of more libraries, nursing homes, and hospitals; (11) hospital insurance for older U.S. citizens "financed by every worker and his employer under Social Security, contributing no more than $1 a month during the employee's working career to protect him in his old age in a dignified manner without cost to the Treasury, against the devastating hardship of prolonged or repeated illness"; (12) "more help to those displaced by slum clearance, provide more housing for our poor and our elderly, and seek as our ultimate goal in our free enterprise system a decent home for every American family"; and (13) the release of "$11 billion of tax reduction into the private spending stream to create new jobs and new markets in every

area of this land." See Johnson, *Public Papers of the Presidents of the United States*, 1:704–7.

14. "President Lyndon B. Johnson's Annual Message to Congress on the State of the Union, January 8, 1964." See Johnson, *Public Papers of the Presidents of the United States*, 1:112–18.

15. Amartya Sen dwells on the concept of capabilities to underline the importance of preconditions for full participation in society as the only fully developed model of development. Amartya Sen, *Development as Freedom* (New York: Knopf, 1999).

16. President Johnson at the Signing of the Independence of Medicare Bill, July 30, 1965. Lyndon B. Johnson, *Public Papers of the Presidents of the United States: Lyndon B. Johnson, 1963–1964*, vol. 2 (Washington, DC: Government Printing Office, 1966), 811–15.

17. David Zarefsky, *President Johnson's War on Poverty: Rhetoric and History* (Tuscaloosa: University of Alabama Press, 2005), 20.

18. Katz, *The Undeserving Poor*, 93.

19. George Axtelle to President Johnson, May 5, 1964, Box 33, Subject File WE-9; White House Central Files (WHCF), Lyndon Baines Johnson Presidential Library, Austin, TX.

20. Jean Ensign to President Johnson, telegram, April 20, 1964, Box 33, WE-9, WHCF, Johnson Library.

21. George Freedley to President Johnson, June 24, 1964, Box 33, WE-9, WHCF, Johnson Library.

22. For more on Johnson's early adulthood, see Robert Caro, *Master of the Senate: The Years of Lyndon Johnson* (New York: Vintage Press, 2003).

23. Father John Wagner to President Johnson, January 10, 1964, Box 32, WE-9, WHCF, Johnson Library.

24. Ernest Sandoval to President Johnson, July 21, 1964, Box 34, WE-9, WHCF, Johnson Library.

25. Bill Lea to President Johnson, March 18, 1964, Box 33, WE-9, WHCF, Johnson Library.

26. William Hurst to President Johnson, April 16, 1964, Box 33, WE-9, WHCF, Johnson Library.

27. Kenneth West to President Johnson, May 8, 1964, Box 33, WE-9, WHCF, Johnson Library.

28. Moyers served as a trusted advisor to Presidents Kennedy and Johnson before going on to a successful career in journalism.

29. George Kramer to President Johnson, March 27, 1964; Box 33, WE-9, WHCF, Johnson Library.

30. Lou Gross to Walter Jenkins, March 10, 1964, Box33, WE-9, WHCF, Johnson Library.

31. Coke Lambert to President Johnson, July 25, 1964; Box 34, WE-9, WHCF, Johnson Library.

32. George Beto to President Johnson, March 17, 1964, Box 126, Subject File FG-11-15, WHCF, Johnson Library.

33. Valenti went on to become the head of the Motion Picture Association.

34. Letter; Ethel Brosius to Jack Valenti, [no date], Box 33, WE-9, WHCF, Johnson Library.

35. Harold Van Coops to President Johnson, [no date], Box 34, WE-9, WHCF, Johnson Library.

36. Conducted by Gallup Organization, October 8–13, 1965, and based on personal interviews with a national adult sample of 2,402.

37. Data from Louis Harris & Associates poll conducted in August 1966 and based on personal interviews with a national adult sample of 1,250.

38. Mr. and Mrs. R. Carroll to George Reedy, May 20, 1965, Box 127, FG-11-15, WHCF, Johnson Library.

39. Anonymous to President Johnson, January 10, 1967, Box 127, FG-11-15, WHCF, Johnson Library.

40. Baxton Bryant to President Johnson, August 24, 1966, Box 127, FG-11-15, WHCF, Johnson Library.

41. Congressmen Augustus Hawkins and Joseph Resnick to President Johnson, telegram, Box 127, FG-11-15, WHCF, Johnson Library.

42. Roger Bell to Mrs. Lyndon Johnson, June 8, 1965, Box 127, FG-11-15, WHCF, Johnson Library.

43. Sumter County Movement for Human Rights to Sargent Shriver, August 8, 1965, Box 127, FG-11-15, WHCF, Johnson Library.

44. Daniel Castro to Rudy Ramos, American GI Forum [copied to Johnson administration], May 20, 1965, Box 127, FG-11-15, WHCF, Johnson Library.

45. Lonnie Johnson to President Johnson, January 11, 1968, Box 127, FG-11-15, WHCF, Johnson Library.

46. N. Eldridge to President Johnson, telegram, March 16, 1966, Box 127, FG-11-15, WHCF, Johnson Library.

47. William Larregui to President Johnson, telegram, Apr. 14, 1966, Box 127, FG-11-15, WHCF, Johnson Library.

48. Paul Kruezenstein to President Johnson, May 13, 1966, Box 127, FG-11-15, WHCF, Johnson Library.

49. Kornbluh details the history of the welfare rights movement all over the United States as it burgeoned into a voice of protest on behalf of recipients. From New York City to Cleveland, from Louisville to Los Angeles, marchers took to the streets to demand an increase in the size of welfare grants, mechanisms for resolving complaints, and a larger voice in the politics of poverty policy. See Felicia Kornbluh, *The Battle for Welfare Rights: Politics and Poverty in Modern America* (Philadelphia: University of Pennsylvania Press, 2007). See also Annelise Orleck, *Storming Caesar's Palace: How Black Mothers Fought Their Own War on Poverty* (Boston: Beacon Press, 2005).

50. Jonathan Bean, "'Burn, Baby, Burn': Small Business in the Urban Riots of the 1960s," *The Independent Review*, 5, no. 2 (2000): 165.

51. Walter [last name illegible] to President Johnson, December 1, 1965, Box 10, Subject File FI-2, WHCF, Johnson Library.

52. Jean Gettle to President Johnson, December 1965, Box 10, FI-2, WHCF, Johnson Library.

53. Mrs. R. B. King to President Johnson, December 2, 1965, Box 10, FI-2, WHCF, Johnson Library.

54. President Lyndon B. Johnson's Annual Message to the Congress on the State of the Union, January 12, 1966. Johnson, *Public Papers of the Presidents of the United States*, 2:3–12, National Archives at College Park, MD.

55. Data from the National Opinion Research Center/Stamford University during February 1966 and based on personal interviews with a national adult sample of 1,474.

56. "President Lyndon B. Johnson's Annual Message to the Congress on the State of the Union, January 14, 1968." Johnson, *Public Papers of the*

Presidents of the United States, 2:1263–70, National Archives at College Park, MD.

57. Gilens, *Why Americans Hate Welfare*.

58. Poll conducted by Louis Harris & Associates, June 1971, with a national sample of 1,600 adults.

59. Elizabethan poor laws directed against the Irish as well as Victorian attitudes toward paupers share the same sentiment: the poor are not deserving by nature, and their genetic makeup explains their indolence.

60. Brock, *Welfare, Democracy, and the New Deal*, 166.

61. Bremner, "The New Deal and Social Welfare," 75. While the poor as a group have always incurred a special stigma, the New Deal was not without serious racial fault lines. Sociologist Jill Quadagno argues that "race has always been the defining feature of the welfare state," and suggests that Roosevelt's New Deal had less to do with maintaining class divisions than with maintaining racial segregation. Occupational restrictions built into eligibility legislation insured the exclusion of many African American workers, and the important role for states in setting relief benefits and rules allowed southern states to systematically exclude African Americans from the basic promise of economic security suggested by the New Deal rhetoric. See Quadagno, *The Color of Welfare*. See also Katznelson, *When Affirmative Action Was White*.

62. See Katz, *The Undeserving Poor*.

63. Daniel Patrick Moynihan, *The Negro Family: The Case for National Action* (Washington, DC: Office of Policy Planning and Research, U.S. Department of Labor, March 1965) (http://www.blackpast.org/?q=primary/moynihan-report-1965).

64. Lee Rainwater and William Yancey, writing a few years later to assess the fallout from the Moynihan Report, noted, "we have in our files eleven articles that appeared in the two weeks between August 16th and September 1st [1965] which relate the Moynihan Report or the breakdown of the Negro family to the Watts riots." Lee Rainwater and William Yancey, *The Moynihan Report and the Politics of Controversy* (Cambridge, MA: MIT Press, 1967), 192.

65. Gilens argues that while Watts and the other urban riots did not directly contribute to a negative shift in whites' racial attitudes at this time,

they did help bring the black urban poor to the forefront of American social problems. See Gilens, *Why Americans Hate Welfare.*

66. In addition, many believed welfare was a prime culprit behind inflation. A 1970 Harris poll found that 68% of the respondents thought welfare and relief payments were contributing to inflation. Thirty-nine percent thought welfare and relief payments were a major cause of inflation, while 29% thought they were a minor cause. Only 22% dismissed this idea. Poll conducted by Louis Harris & Associates during February 1970 and based on personal interviews with a national adult sample of 1,600.

67. Daniel Moynihan to President Nixon, memo, March 13, 1969; Box 39, Staff Member and Office Files (SMOF), John D. Ehrlichman; White House Special Files (WHSF), Richard Nixon Presidential Library and Museum, National Archives at College Park, MD.

68. The proposed income floor would vary over the next two years as the FAP made its unsuccessful way through Congress.

69. "Address to the Nation on Domestic Programs," August 8, 1969, in *Public Papers of the Presidents: Richard Nixon, 1969,* 639–45, National Archives at College Park, MD.

70. Quadagno, *The Color of Welfare,* 118.

71. Milton Friedman, *Capitalism and Freedom* (Chicago: University of Chicago Press, 2002 [1962]). In this signature volume, Friedman argued that the fluctuations of income among low-income families could be smoothed with a negative income tax.

72. Daniel Patrick Moynihan, *The Politics of a Guaranteed Income: The Nixon Administration and the Family Assistance Plan* (New York: Random House, 1973), 245.

73. See Brian Steensland, *The Failed Welfare Revolution: America's Struggle over Guaranteed Income Policy* (Princeton, NJ: Princeton University Press, 2007).

74. John Ehrlichman to Elliot Richardson, memo, April 21, 1971, Box 7, Subject File WE, White House Central File (WHCF), Nixon Library, National Archives at College Park, MD.

75. H. R. Haldeman to Ed Morgan, memo, May 4, 1971, Box 7, WE, WHCF, Nixon Library, National Archives at College Park, MD.

76. See Quadagno, *The Color of Welfare,* 118.

77. Quadagno, *The Color of Welfare*, 123. In his in-depth interviews with Jewish and Italian Brooklynites, sociologist Jonathan Rieder identifies similar sentiments among these white working-class respondents, who felt the welfare "system seems to encourage multigenerational welfare families, undermining the public's trust in eventual symbolic or material repayment." See Jonathan Rieder, *Canarsie: The Jews and Italians of Brooklyn against Liberalism* (Cambridge, MA: Harvard University Press, 1985), 106.

78. Brendan Sexton, "Workers and Liberals: Closing the Gap," in *The White Majority: Between Poverty and Affluence*, ed. L. K. Howe (New York: Random House, 1970), 232.

79. Richard Lemon, *The Troubled American* (New York: Simon & Schuster, 1971), 33.

80. Martin Anderson to President Nixon, memo, January 20, 1970, Box 7, WE, WHCF, Nixon Library, National Archives at College Park, MD.

81. Patrick Buchanan to John Ehrlichman, memo, February 3, 1971, Box 7, WE, WHCF, Nixon Library, National Archives at College Park, MD.

82. Similar meetings continued to be held with "minority group members in an attempt to secure their support for Welfare Reform. It is very clear that there is a moderate minority group that is concerned about Welfare Reform and under the proper circumstances could give the Administration the support it needs." "The only minority voice that is speaking out on Welfare Reform is Dr. George Wiley's National Welfare Rights Organization. They are definitely opposed to the present legislation and are also opposed to this Administration. Thus, it is quite important to the President that we develop a strategy that will bring about support from the minority community." Elliot Richardson to John Ehrlichman, memo, April 23, 1971, Box 7, WE, WHCF, Nixon Library, National Archives at College Park, MD.

83. Daniel Moynihan to Ken Cole, memo, September 17, 1969, Box 39, SMOF Ehrlichman, WHSF, Nixon Library, National Archives at College Park, MD.

84. John Ehrlichman to President Nixon, September 17, 1969, Box 39, SMOF Ehrlichman, WHSF, Nixon Library, National Archives at College Park, MD.

85. Daniel Moynihan to President Nixon, January 20, 1970, Box 38, SMOF Ehrlichman, WHSF, Nixon Library, National Archives at College Park, MD.

86. See Steensland, *The Failed Welfare Revolution*.

87. Bruce Blackmon to President Nixon, January 28, 1969, Box 13, WE, WHCF, Nixon Library, National Archives at College Park, MD.

88. Mrs. John C. Hanson to Daniel Moynihan, February 5, 1969, Box 13, WE, WHCF, Nixon Library, National Archives at College Park, MD.

89. Mrs. J. F. Landis to President Nixon, May 20, 1969, Box 13, WE, WHCF, Nixon Library, National Archives at College Park, MD.

90. Joseph L. Carbo to John Ehrlichman, February 2, 1972, Box 21, WE, WHCF, Nixon Library, National Archives at College Park, MD.

91. D. L. Millroy to Daniel Moynihan, February 4, 1969, Box 13, WE, WHCF, Nixon Library, National Archives at College Park, MD.

92. Mrs. Chas Stephens to John Ehrlichman, October 5, 1971, Box 20, WE, WHCF, Nixon Library, National Archives at College Park, MD.

93. Joseph L. Carbo to John Ehrlichman, February 2, 1972, Box 21, WE, WHCF, Nixon Library, National Archives at College Park, MD.

94. Mrs. J. F. Landis to President Nixon, May 20, 1969, Box 13, WE, WHCF, Nixon Library, National Archives at College Park, MD.

95. Mrs. Walter H. Wiese to Congressman Lamar Baker, April 21, 1971, Box 62, WE, WHCF, Nixon Library, National Archives at College Park, MD.

96. Mrs. F. H. Sherman to Congressman J. Irving Whaley, October 13, 1969, Box 62, WE, WHCF, Nixon Library, National Archives at College Park, MD.

97. Joseph L. Carbo to John Ehrlichman, February 2, 1972, Box 21, WE, WHCF, Nixon Library, National Archives at College Park, MD.

98. Mrs. John C. Hanson to Daniel Moynihan, February 5, 1969, Box 13, WE, WHCF, Nixon Library, National Archives at College Park, MD.

99. Mrs. J. F. Landis to President Nixon, May 20, 1969, Box 13, WE, WHCF, Nixon Library, National Archives at College Park, MD.

100. Jim DeLapa to President Nixon, January 5, 1971, Box 20, WE, WHCF, Nixon Library, National Archives at College Park, MD.

101. R. L. Smith to Daniel Moynihan, February 5, 1969, Box 13, WE,WHCF, Nixon Library, National Archives at College Park, MD.

102. Marshall Alston to President Nixon, February 5, 1969, Box 13, WE 9, WHCF, Nixon Library, National Archives at College Park, MD.

103. Eleven Utah Residents to President Nixon, May 13, 1969, Box 62, WE 9, WHCF, Nixon Library, National Archives at College Park, MD.

104. Quoted in a National Federation of Independent Businesses press release that was forwarded to the White House Director of Communications. Enclosed in letter; Herbert Klein to Niel Heard, July 23, 1970, Box 63, WE; WHCF, Nixon Library, National Archives at College Park, MD.

105. Arthur Burns to President Nixon, memo, April 28, 1969, Box 60, WE, WHCF, Nixon Library, National Archives at College Park, MD. Note that nonwhites supported the plan and at an increasing rate (66%, 73%), and families earning less than $3,000 were split evenly.

106. Eleanor Garrett to President Nixon, January 27, 1969, Box 13, WE, WHCF, Nixon Library, National Archives at College Park, MD. The letters in this section predated the August announcement, but were written with the knowledge that the administration was devising a guaranteed income plan.

107. Doris L. Picard to President Nixon, June 12, 1969, Box 62, WE, WHCF, Nixon Library, National Archives at College Park, MD.

108. Eugene F. Tinker to John Ehrlichman, March 31, 1970; Box 63, WE, WHCF, Nixon Library, National Archives at College Park, MD.

109. Mrs. Walter H. Wiese to Congressman Lamar Baker, April 21, 1971, Box 62, WE, WHCF, Nixon Library, National Archives at College Park, MD. Emphasis in original.

110. Agnes Royce to Daniel Moynihan, July 28, 1970, Box 63, WE, WHCF, Nixon Library, National Archives at College Park, MD.

111. John Fandrich to Daniel Moynihan, February 5, 1969, Box 13, WE, WHCF, Nixon Library, National Archives at College Park, MD.

112. William K. Phillips to Daniel Moynihan, May 20, 1969, Box 62, WE, WHCF, Nixon Library, National Archives at College Park, MD.

113. W. D. Johnson to President Nixon, February 24, 1972, Box 21, WE, WHCF, Nixon Library, National Archives at College Park, MD. Emphasis in original.

114. David Cheses to Daniel Moynihan, May 7, 1969, Box 62, WE, WHCF, Nixon Library, National Archives at College Park, MD.

115. Kenneth R. McIntyre to President Nixon, May 15, 1969, Box 62, WE, WHCF, Nixon Library, National Archives at College Park, MD.

116. C. P. Bennett to Daniel Moynihan, May 27, 1969, Box 62, WE, WHCF, Nixon Library, National Archives at College Park, MD.

117. Arch Booth to President Nixon, April 3, 1970, Box 61, WE, WHCF, Nixon Library, National Archives at College Park, MD.

118. Piven and Cloward, *Regulating the Poor*, 3.

119. For more on the history and impact of the EITC, see Steve Holt, "The Earned Income Tax Credit at Age 30: What We Know," research brief for the Metropolitan Policy Program at Brookings Institution, February 2006.

120. See Steensland, *The Failed Welfare Revolution*.

CHAPTER 3

1. David Brooks, "The American Way of Equality," *New York Times*, January 14, 2007.

2. Alan Greenspan, testimony before the Joint Economic Committee of the U.S. Congress, June 9, 2005.

3. As quoted in *Waging a Living: Tales of the Poor, Working to Survive in America*, a documentary film directed by Roger Weisberg and Pamela Harris (Public Policy Productions, 2005).

4. See Daniel Gross, "Plutocrats of the People: Why Are America's Superrich Suddenly Fretting about Inequality?" *Slate*, January 19, 2007 (http://www.slate.com/id/2157859/).

5. Todd Purdham, "Electoral Affirmation of Shared Values Provides Bush a Majority," *New York Times*, November 4, 2004.

6. Jodie T. Allen and Michael Dimock, "A Nation of 'Haves' and 'Have-Nots'? Far More Americans Now See Their Country as Sharply Divided along Economic Lines" (Washington, DC: Pew Research Center for the People & the Press, September 13, 2007) (http://pewresearch.org/pubs/593/haves-have-nots).

7. Gibson's remarks came during a 2008 Democratic presidential debate between candidates Hillary Clinton and Barack Obama. Senator Clinton was arguing for the expiration of tax cuts on the wealthy and the continuation of tax cuts for the middle class. Mr. Gibson replied, "If you take a family of two professors here at Saint Anselm [College], they're going to

be in that $200,000 category that you're talking about lifting the taxes on." See a transcription of the debate at http://www.2008electionprocon.org/pdf/ Dem20080105.pdf.

8. According to the U.S. Census.

9. While data limitations prohibit analyses of the U.S. Census to examine the very top of the income distribution, economists Emmanuel Saez and Thomas Piketty have combed through Internal Revenue Service and Social Security Administration data that allow for a more complete picture of the top end of the income distribution. Those data are available online at Saez's website, http://elsa.berkely.edu/~saez/.

10. Claudia Goldin and Robert A. Margo, "The Great Compression: The U.S. Wage Structure at Mid-Century," *Quarterly Journal of Economics* 107 (1992): 1.

11. At the 20th percentile of the income distribution.

12. At the 80th percentile of the income distribution.

13. Thomas Piketty and Emanuel Saez, "Income Inequality in the United States, 1913–1998," *Quarterly Journal of Economics* 118, no. 1 (2003): 1–39. Tables and figures have been updated to 2006 at http://elsa. berkely.edu/~saez/.

14. Carola Frydman and Raven E. Saks, "Executive Compensation: A New View from a Long-Term Perspective, 1935–2005." FEDS Working Paper No. 2007-35, July 6, 2007. Presented at the AFA meeting, New Orleans, 2008 (http://ssrn.com/abstract=972399).

15. Louis Uchitelle, "The Richest of the Rich, Proud in a New Gilded Age," *New York Times*, July 15, 2007.

16. David Card and John E. DiNardo, "Skill-Biased Technological Change and Rising Wage Inequality: Some Problems and Puzzles." *Journal of Labor Economics* 20, no. 4 (2002): 733.

17. Robert H. Frank and Phillip J. Cook, *The Winner-Take-All Society: Why the Few at the Top Get So Much More Than the Rest of Us* (New York: Penguin, 1996).

18. Paul Krugman, "For Richer," *New York Times Sunday Magazine*, October 20, 2002.

19. "Inequality in America," *The Economist*, June 15, 2006.

20. Everett Carl Ladd and Karlyn Bowman, *Attitudes Toward Economic Inequality* (Washington, DC: American Enterprise Institute, 1998).

21. Andrew Hacker, *Money: Who Has How Much and Why* (New York: Simon & Schuster, 1999).

22. These data come from the 1999 wave of the International Social Survey Project (ISSP), a cross-national survey of attitudes that collected responses from a nationally representative sample of individuals in ten countries with roughly comparable economies.

23. Alexis de Toqueville, *Democracy in America* (Chicago: University of Chicago Press, 2000 [1835]).

24. Stanley Feldman, cited in Larry M. Bartels, *Unequal Democracy: The Political Economy of the New Gilded Age* (Princeton, NJ: Princeton University Press, 2008).

25. Jennifer Hochschild, *What's Fair? American Beliefs about Distributive Justice* (Cambridge, MA: Harvard University Press, 1981).

26. Bartels, *Unequal Democracy.*

27. For example, the percentage of Americans favoring a law against interracial marriage has decreased from 37% in the early 1970s to just 10% in 2002. The percentage of Americans disapproving of the idea of a woman working outside the home has decreased from 33% in 1972 to 18% in 1998. See the General Social Survey for more on changing social attitudes (http://www.norc.org/GSS).

28. Past studies focusing on tolerance for economic inequality have relied heavily on data on other topics, including individual opportunity (e.g., whether success is determined by hard work, luck, discrimination, individual ability, connections, etc.), and preferences for redistribution. The vast majority of the survey questions probing attitudes over time were devised during a period when other forms of inequality were of far greater interest to survey researchers, with a particular focus on racial and gender equality. As one author notes, "the conceptual fit between beliefs about income inequality and existing questions about opportunity and redistribution may not be as tight as we would like for the period of rising income inequality in the United States." See Leslie McCall, "The Undeserving Rich: Beliefs about Inequality in the Era of Rising Inequality" (Evanston, IL: Institute for Policy Research, Northwestern University, October 11, 2007).

29. These data represent the most comprehensive time-series data on attitudes toward economic inequality in the United States. The GSS is a nationally-representative survey, with more than 1,000 respondents offering

answers on the relevant questions. These data are characterized by several weaknesses worth mentioning. First, the 1987 start date of the time series is more than a decade into the period of rising economic inequality. Second, the absence of data from the period of sustained economic growth and low inequality between the end of the Second World War and the early 1970s means that we have no clear basis of comparison of attitudes before and after a high degree of inequality characterized the American economy. Third, the data provide only a handful of points in time, rather than an annual time series that would allow for deeper exploration of continuity and change. Nonetheless, the data do allow us to trace attitudes during a period of rising inequality, and they represent the best that we have.

30. "Too high" is defined as answering either "agree" or "strongly agree."

31. Specifically, we take the standard deviation of the respondent's perception of fair wages and divide this by the mean of the distribution in order to compute a measure of a respondent's perception of a fair level of inequality (FAIR). We repeat this process for the respondent's perception of actual wages, generating a measure of a respondent's perception of the actual level of inequality (ACTUAL). We regress FAIR on ACTUAL to obtain a standardized residual, which captures a respondent's preference for wage redistribution (WAGE), a proxy for his level of dissatisfaction with current levels of inequality. Including ACTUAL in the calculation of WAGE is critical not only because of high levels of correlation between ACTUAL and FAIR, but also for the intuitive reason that we should expect an individual's perception of a fair wage distribution to be strongly conditioned on his or her understanding of the actual economic distribution, and thus his or her desire for redistribution as well.

32. McCall, "The Undeserving Rich."

33. McCall notes, however, that the 2000 values for both of these indicators fall back to their 1987 levels. See McCall, "The Undeserving Rich."

34. See Katherine S. Newman *Declining Fortunes: The Withering of the American Dream* (New York: Basic Books, 1993), 2002, for a discussion of the cultural contours of generations as they are defined by labor market entry.

35. Note that the results are not sensitive to the precise composition of birth cohort. Analyses varying the years for inclusion in each cohort returned consistent results.

36. Other variables included in our model are income, education, subjective social class, gender, union status, self-employment status, and a

variable capturing an individual's relative skills specificity. The relative skills specificity variable draws on the work of Torben Iversen and David Soskice, who provide compelling evidence suggesting individuals' economic attitudes are strongly influenced by the specificity of their skill set. Those with highly specific skill sets are likely to differ in their economic preferences from those with more general skill sets, as those with specific skill sets are likely to view their economic prospects as more limited. See Torben Iversen and David Soskice, "An Asset Theory of Social Policy Preferences," *American Political Science Review* 95, no. 4 (2001): 875–93.

37. McCall's work on attitudes toward income inequality complements our analysis. In short, she argues, across a variety of measures capturing basic attitudes toward economic inequality, "the time trend remains strong and positive throughout the series of models that control for family income, education, other demographic and individual characteristics, subjective class, perceived opportunity for mobility, partisan ideology and identification." See McCall, "The Undeserving Rich."

38. See Thomas Byrne Edsall and Mary D. Edsall, *Chain Reaction: The Impact of Race, Rights, and Taxes on American Politics* (New York: Norton, 1991).

39. Edsall and Edsall, *Chain Reaction*, 202.

40. Katz, *The Undeserving Poor*, 183.

41. Rieder, *Canarsie*, 101.

42. Skocpol, "Targeting Within Universalism, 419.

43. Edsall and Edsall, *Chain Reaction*, 205.

44. Charles Noble, *Welfare As We Knew It: A Political History of the American Welfare State* (New York: Oxford University Press, 1997), 114.

45. Thomas Byrne Edsall, *The New Politics of Inequality* (New York: Norton, 1994), 213.

46. Frances Fox Piven and Richard Cloward, *The New Class War: Reagan's Attack on the Welfare State and Its Consequences* (New York: Pantheon, 1982), 6.

47. Ibid, 10.

48. Katz, *In the Shadow of the Poorhouse*, 278.

49. Stephen Pimpare, *The New Victorians: Poverty, Politics, and Propaganda in Two Gilded Ages* (New York: New Press, 2004), 4–10.

50. Katz, *The Undeserving Poor*, 142–76.

51. Fay Lomax Cook and Edith J. Barrett, *Support for the American Welfare State: The Views of Congress and the Public* (New York: Columbia University Press, 1992), 27.

52. I. A. Lewis and William Schneider, "Hard Times: The Public on Poverty," *Public Opinion*, June/July 1985, 79.

53. Ibid.

54. Ibid.

55. See Linda Bennett and Stephen Bennett, *Living with Leviathan: Americans Coming to Terms with Big Government* (Lawrence: University of Kansas Press, 1990), 80.

56. Lawrence Bobo and Ryan Smith, "Antipoverty Policy, Affirmative Action, and Racial Attitudes," in *Confronting Poverty: Prescriptions for Change*, ed. S. Danziger, G. Sandefur, and D.Weinberg (Cambridge, MA: Harvard University Press, 1994), 367.

57. Jeffry Will, *The Deserving Poor* (New York: Garland Publishing, 1993), 100.

58. Similarly, AuClaire finds that the opinion polls "strongly suggest that 'welfare backlash,' although present to some degree, is neither as intensely felt nor is the concept as widely supported as one might have expected" given the public rhetoric swirling around the programs. See Philip Arthur AuClair, "Public Attitudes toward Social Welfare Expenditures," *Social Work*, March/April 1984, 139. Hendrickson and Axelrod polled 200-plus middle-class respondents in 1983 regarding their attitudes about the work ethic, poverty, and social policy. They conclude that while the "overwhelming majority" expressed agreements with values represented by the work ethic, a majority cited "the economic system" as opposed to a "characterological explanation for poverty," and "endorse social welfare programs that call for a wide variety of strategies to address poverty." See Robert Hendrickson and Leland Axelrod, "Middle-Class Attitudes Toward the Poor: Are They Changing?" *Social Service Review*, June 1985, 295.

59. Steven Teles, *Whose Welfare? AFDC and Elite Politics* (Lawrence: University Press of Kansas, 1996), 44.

60. R. Kent Weaver, *Ending Welfare as We Know It* (Washington, DC: Brookings Institution Press, 2000), 171.

61. The Role of Government Module of the GSS asked respondents a battery of questions regarding the appropriate role of government in a

variety of realms, including specific questions pertaining to government's appropriate role in reducing economic disparities, as well as preferred levels of government spending in a variety of social welfare–related fields. The survey was fielded in 1985, 1990, and 1996, and thus affords a glimpse of attitudes across a period of rising inequality, including attitudes in the wake of the overhaul of welfare in the mid-1990s.

62. See Jacob S. Hacker, *The Great Risk Shift* (New York: Oxford University Press, 2006).

63. See Jared Bernstein, *Crunch: Why Do I Feel So Squeezed (And Other Economic Mysteries)* (San Francisco: Berrett-Koehler Publishers, 2008).

CHAPTER 4

1. See Steensland, *The Failed Welfare Revolution.*

2. See Jeffrey Liebman's overview of the EITC, including a review of the relationship between FAP and EITC. Jeffrey B. Liebman, "The Impact of the Earned Income Tax Credit on Incentives and Income," in *Tax Policy and the Economy*, ed. James Poterba (Cambridge, MA: MIT Press, 1998).

3. John Zaller, *The Nature and Origins of Mass Opinion* (Cambridge: Cambridge University Press, 1992).

4. See, e.g., James A. Stimson, *Public Opinion in America: Moods, Cycles, and Swings* (Boulder, CO: Westview Press, 1999). See also Robert S. Erikson, M. B. Mackuen, and J. A. Stimson, *The Macropolity* (Cambridge: Cambridge University Press, 2008).

5. V. O. Key, *Public Opinion and American Democracy* (New York: Knopf, 1961).

6. John Zaller, "Coming to Grips with V. O. Key's Concept of Latent Public Opinion," paper delivered at the Symposium in Honor of Phillip Converse, Boston, September 2, 1998, 13.

7. Like the dynamic and responsive nature of public opinion, the concept of rational, coherent, and stable public opinion is a well-documented concept grounded in a rich literature. In particular, Benjamin I. Page and Robert Y. Shapiro's seminal *The Rational Public: Fifty Years of Americans' Policy Preferences* (Chicago: University of Chicago Press, 1992) offers a cogent argument in support of the idea that the American public "as a collectivity, holds a number of real, stable, and sensible opinions about public

policy, and that these opinions develop and change in a reasonable fashion, responding to changing circumstances and to new information."

8. Caro, *Master of the Senate*.

9. Achen and Bartels, "Partisan Hearts and Gall Bladders."

10. The exception was the Great Society's medical care programs of Medicaid and Medicare. Medicaid represented a true reach, as it offered health insurance to the poor—many of whom were nonworkers and therefore out of the bounds of the American concept of desert. Medicare, however, was similarly couched in the language of deserving, as it was built around Social Security taxes paid by working Americans, and the selling point was that government was simply helping working Americans provide a safety net for *themselves*.

11. At least two Clinton administration officials quit because of their frustration with the president's approach to welfare policy. See Barbara Vobejda and Judith Havemann, "2 HHS Officials Quit Over Welfare Changes," *Washington Post*, September 12, 1996.

12. See Mark Greenberg and Lisa Donner, "Stalled Progress on Poverty" (Washington, DC: Center for American Progress, August 26, 2008; http://www.americanprogress.org/issues/2008/08/stalled_progress.html). Greenberg and Donner refer to the U.S. Census for poverty figures.

13. Rockfeller Brothers Foundation/Time Campaign for America's Workers Survey, 2008. This survey was fielded before the financial crisis sent the economy into a tailspin, making its respondents' gloomy outlook all the more distressing.

14. As cited by Julia B. Isaacs and Isabel V. Sawhill, "Getting Ahead or Losing Ground? Economic Mobility in America," Economic Mobility Project of the Pew Charitable Trusts, Washington, DC, 2008.

15. Jacob S. Hacker and Elisabeth S. Jacobs, "The Rising Instability of American Family Incomes, 1969–2004," briefing paper for the Economic Policy Institute, Washington, DC, 2008.

16. Henry Farber, "Job Loss and the Decline of Job Security in the United States," Working Paper No. 520 (Princeton, NJ: Industrial Relations Section, Princeton University, 2007).

17. Ibid.

18. Elisabeth S. Jacobs and Katherine S. Newman, "Rising Angst? Change and Stability in Perceptions of Economic Instability," in *Laid Off,*

Laid Low: The Social and Political Consequences of Job Instability (New York: Columbia University Press, 2008).

19. Isaacs and Sawhill, "Getting Ahead or Losing Ground?"

20. Farber, "Job Loss and the Decline of Job Security in the United States."

21. Kaiser Family Foundation, "Health Coverage and the Uninsured" (http://www.kff.org/uninsured/index.cfm).

22. See, e.g., Newman, *Falling from Grace*, and many others.

23. Robert H. Frank, *Falling Behind: How Rising Inequality Harms the Middle Class* (Berkeley and Los Angeles: University of California Press, 2007).

24. Kenneth F. Scheve and Matthew J. Slaughter, "A New Deal for Globalization," *Foreign Affairs*, July/August 2007.

25. Lawrence Summers, "Unfinished Business at Fannie Mae and Freddie Mac," *Washington Post*, July 27, 2008.

26. Note that neither Roosevelt nor Johnson paid a political price for moving out in front of the public with their social welfare policies. Both were reelected multiple times with substantial margins of victory.

Bibliography

Achen, Christopher, and Larry Bartels, "Partisan Hearts and Gall Bladders: Retrospection and Realignment in the Wake of the Great Depression." Presented at the Midwest Political Science Association Annual Meeting, Chicago, April 7–9, 2007.

Allen, Jodie T., and Michael Dimock. "A Nation of 'Haves' and 'Have-Nots'? Far More Americans Now See Their Country as Sharply Divided Along Economic Lines." Washington, DC: Pew Research Center for the People & the Press, September 13, 2007. http://pewresearch.org/pubs/593/haves-have-nots.

Amenta, Edwin. *Bold Relief: Institutional Politics and the Origins of Modern American Social Policy.* Princeton, NJ: Princeton University Press, 1998.

———. *When Movements Matter: The Townsend Plan and the Rise of Social Security.* Princeton, NJ: Princeton University Press, 2006.

Angell, Robert. *The Family Encounters the Depression.* New York: Scribner's Sons, 1936.

AuClair, Philip Arthur. "Public Attitudes Toward Social Welfare Expenditures." *Social Work,* March/April 1984.

Bakke, E. Wight. *The Unemployed Worker: A Study of the Task of Making a Living Without a Job.* Hamden, CT: Archon Books, 1969 [1940].

Balderrama, F. E., and R. Rodriguez. *Decade of Betrayal: Mexican Repatriation in the 1930s.* Albuquerque: University of New Mexico Press, 1995.

Bartels, Larry M. *Unequal Democracy: The Political Economy of the New Gilded Age.* Princeton, NJ: Princeton University Press, 2008.

Baum, Matthew A., and Samuel Kernell. "Economic Class and Popular Support for Franklin Roosevelt in War and Peace." *Public Opinion Quarterly* 65 (2001): 198–229.

Bean, Jonathan. "'Burn, Baby, Burn': Small Business in the Urban Riots of the 1960s" *The Independent Review* 5, no. 2 (2000): 165.

Bennett, Linda, and Stephen Bennett. *Living with Leviathan: Americans Coming to Terms with Big Government*. Lawrence: University of Kansas Press, 1990.

Berinsky, Adam. "American Public Opinion in the 1930s and 1940s: The Analysis of Quota-Controlled Sample Survey Data." *Public Opinion Quarterly* 70, no. 4 (2006): 499.

Bernstein, Irving. *The Lean Years: A History of the American Workers, 1920–1933*. Boston: Houghton Mifflin, 1972.

Bernstein, Jared. *Crunch: Why Do I Feel So Squeezed (And Other Economic Mysteries)*. San Francisco: Berrett-Koehler Publishers, 2008.

Bobo, Lawrence, and Ryan Smith. "Antipoverty Policy, Affirmative Action, and Racial Attitudes." In *Confronting Poverty: Prescriptions for Change*, ed. S. Danziger, G. Sandefur and D.Weinberg. Cambridge, MA: Harvard University Press, 1994.

Bremner, Robert. "The New Deal and Social Welfare." In *Fifty Years Later: The New Deal Evaluated*, ed. Harvard Sitkoff. New York: Knopf, 1984.

Brinkley, Alan. *Voices of Protest: Huey Long, Father Coughlin, and the Great Depression*. New York: Vintage Books, 1983.

Brock, William. *Welfare, Democracy and the New Deal*. New York: Cambridge University Press, 1988.

Brooks, Clem, and Jeff Manza. *Why Welfare States Persist: The Importance of Public Opinion in Democracies*. Chicago: University of Chicago Press, 2007.

Brooks, David. "The American Way of Equality." *New York Times*, January 14, 2007.

Brown, Josephine Chapin. *Public Relief: 1929–1939*. New York: Holt, Rinehardt and Winston, 1940.

Cantril, Hadley, and Mildred Strunk. *Public Opinion 1935–1946*. Princeton, NJ: Princeton University Press, 1951.

Card, David, and John E. DiNardo. "Skill-Biased Technological Change and Rising Wage Inequality: Some Problems and Puzzles." *Journal of Labor Economics* 20, no. 4 (2002): 733.

Caro, Robert. *Master of the Senate: The Years of Lyndon Johnson*. New York: Vintage Press, 2003.

Carter, Boake. *Johnny Q Public Speaks! The Nation Appraises the New Deal*. New York: Dodge Publishing Co., 1936.

Cavan, Ruth, and Katherine Ranck. *The Family and the Depression: A Study of One Hundred Chicago Families*. Chicago: University of Chicago Press, 1938.

Cohen, Lizabeth. *Making a New Deal: Industrial Workers in Chicago, 1919–1939*. New York: Cambridge University Press, 1991.

———. *A Consumers' Republic: The Politics of Mass Consumption in Postwar America*. New York: Vintage, 2003.

Cook, Fay Lomax, and Edith J. Barrett. *Support for the American Welfare State: The Views of Congress and the Public*. New York: Columbia University Press, 1992.

Daniels, Roger. *Guarding the Golden Door: American Immigration Policy and Immigrants Since 1882*. New York: Hill and Wang, 2004.

de Toqueville, Alexis. *Democracy in America*. Chicago: University of Chicago Press, 2000 [1835]).

Dudley, Kathryn. *Debt and Dispossession: Farm Loss in America's Heartland*. Chicago: University of Chicago Press, 2002.

Edsall, Thomas Byrne. *The New Politics of Inequality*. New York: Norton, 1994.

Edsall, Thomas Byrne, and Mary D. Edsall. *Chain Reaction: The Impact of Race, Rights, and Taxes on American Politics*. New York: Norton, 1991.

Erikson, Robert S., M. B. Mackuen and J. A. Stimson. *The Macropolity*. Cambridge: Cambridge University Press, 2008.

Farber, Henry. "Job Loss and the Decline of Job Security in the United States." Working Paper No. 520. Princeton, NJ: Industrial Relations Section, Princeton University, 2007.

Fox, Cybelle. "The Changing Color of Welfare? How Whites' Attitudes Toward Latinos Influence Support for Welfare." *American Journal of Sociology* 110, no. 3 (2004): 580.

———. "Expelling the 'Aliens': The Deportation and Repatriation of Destitute Mexicans and Europeans." Presented at the Social Science History Conference, Chicago, November 2007.

Frank, Robert H. *Falling Behind: How Rising Inequality Harms the Middle Class*. Berkeley and Los Angeles: University of California Press, 2007.

Frank, Robert H., and Phillip J. Cook. *The Winner-Take-All Society: Why the Few at the Top Get So Much More Than the Rest of Us*. New York: Penguin, 1996.

Freeman, Joshua. "Tricky Dick's Legacy: A Review of Rick Perlstein's *Nixonland*," *Dissent*, Summer 2008.

Friedman, Milton. *Capitalism and Freedom*. Chicago: University of Chicago Press, 2002.

Frydman, Carola, and Raven E. Saks, "Executive Compensation: A New View from a Long-Term Perspective, 1935–2005." FEDS Working Paper No. 2007-

35, July 6, 2007. Presented at the AFA meeting, New Orleans, 2008. http://ssrn.com/abstract=972399.

Galbraith, John Kenneth. *The Affluent Society.* Boston: Houghton Mifflin, 1958.

Gilens, Martin. *Why Americans Hate Welfare: Race, Media, and the Politics of Antipoverty Policy.* Chicago: University of Chicago Press, 2000.

Goldberg, Chad Alan. *Citizens and Paupers: Relief, Rights and Race, from the Freedmen's Bureau to Workfare.* Chicago: University of Chicago Press, 2007.

Goldin, Claudia, and Robert A. Margo. "The Great Compression: The U.S. Wage Structure at Mid-Century." *Quarterly Journal of Economics* 107 (1992): 1.

Gordon, Linda. *Pitied But Not Entitled: Single Mothers and the History of Welfare.* Cambridge, MA: Harvard University Press, 1998.

Greenberg, Mark, and Lisa Donner. "Stalled Progress on Poverty." Washington, DC: Center for American Progress, August 26, 2008. http://www.americanprogress.org/issues/2008/08/stalled_progress.html.

Hacker, Andrew. *Money: Who Has How Much and Why.* New York: Simon & Schuster, 1999.

Hacker, Jacob S. *The Great Risk Shift.* New York: Oxford University Press, 2006.

Hacker, Jacob S., and Elisabeth S. Jacobs. "The Rising Instability of American Family Incomes, 1969–2004." Briefing paper for the Economic Policy Institute, Washington, DC, 2008.

Harrington, Michael. *The Other American: Poverty in the United States.* New York: Macmillan, 1962.

Hendrickson, Robert, and Leland Axelrod, "Middle-Class Attitudes Toward the Poor: Are They Changing?" *Social Service Review*, June 1985.

Hochschild, Jennifer. *What's Fair? American Beliefs about Distributive Justice.* Cambridge, MA: Harvard University Press, 1981.

Holt, Steve. "The Earned Income Tax Credit at Age 30: What We Know." Research brief for the Metropolitan Policy Program at the Brookings Institution, February 2006.

Alexander Holzoff, "Some popular misconceptions regarding unemployment compensation." http://www.ssa.gov/history/reports/ces/ces1holtzhoff.html.

Howard, Donald. *The WPA and Federal Relief Policy.* New York: Russell Sage Foundation, 1943.

Igo, Sarah E. *The Averaged American: Surveys, Citizens, and the Making of a Mass Public.* Cambridge, MA: Harvard University Press, 2007.

"Inequality in America." *Economist*, June 17, 2006.

Isaacs, Julia B., and Isabel V. Sawhill. "Getting Ahead or Losing Ground? Economic Mobility in America." Economic Mobility Project of the Pew Charitable Trusts, Washington, DC, 2008.

Iversen, Torben, and David Soskice. "An Asset Theory of Social Policy Preferences." *American Political Science Review* 95, no. 4 (2001): 875–93.

Jacobs, Elisabeth S., and Katherine S. Newman, "Rising Angst? Change and Stability in Perceptions of Economic Instability," in *Laid Off, Laid Low: The Social and Political Consequences of Job Instability*. New York: Columbia University Press, 2008.

Johnson, Lyndon B. *Public Papers of the Presidents of the United States: Lyndon B. Johnson, 1963–1964*, vol. 1. Washington, DC: Government Printing Office, 1965.

———. *Public Papers of the Presidents of the United States: Lyndon B. Johnson, 1963–1964*, vol. 2. Washington, DC: Government Printing Office, 1966.

Katz, Michael B. *In the Shadow of the Poorhouse: A Social History of Welfare in America*. New York: Basic Books, 1986.

———. *The Undeserving Poor: From the War on Poverty to the War on Welfare*. New York: Pantheon, 1989.

Katznelson, Ira. *When Affirmative Action Was White: An Untold History of Racial Inequality in Twentieth-Century America*. New York: W. W. Norton, 2006.

Kessler-Harris, Alice. *In Pursuit of Equity: Women, Men and the Quest for Economic Citizenship in 20th Century America*. New York: Oxford University Press, 2001.

Key, V. O. *Public Opinion and American Democracy*. New York: Knopf, 1961.

Komarovsky, Mirra. *The Unemployed Man and His Family: The Effect of Unemployment Upon the Status of the Man in Fifty-Nine Families*. Lanham, MD: AltaMira Press, 2004 [1940].

Kornbluh, Felicia. *The Battle for Welfare Rights: Politics and Poverty in Modern America*. Philadelphia: University of Pennsylvania Press, 2007.

Krugman, Paul. "For Richer." *New York Times Sunday Magazine*, October 20, 2002.

Ladd, Everett Carl, and Karlyn Bowman. *Attitudes Toward Economic Inequality*. Washington, DC: American Enterprise Institute, 1998.

Lemon, Richard. *The Troubled American*. New York: Simon & Schuster, 1971.

Lewis, I. A., and William Schneider. "Hard Times: The Public on Poverty." *Public Opinion*, June/July 1985.

Liebman, Jeffrey B. "The Impact of the Earned Income Tax Credit on Incentives and Income." In *Tax Policy and the Economy*, ed. James Poterba. Cambridge, MA: MIT Press, 1998.

Lieberman, Robert C. *Shifting the Color Line: Race and the American Welfare State*. Cambridge, MA: Harvard University Press, 2001.

Lynd, Robert S., and Helen Merrell Lynd. *Middletown in Transition: A Study in Cultural Conflicts*. New York: Harcourt Brace Jovanovich, 1982 (1937).

McCall, Leslie. "The Undeserving Rich: Beliefs about Inequality in the Era of Rising Inequality." Institute for Policy Research, Northwestern University, Evanston, IL, October 11, 2007. http://www.northwestern.edu/ipr/publications/papers/mccall/undeservingrich-1007.pdf.

McCarthy, Eugene. *A Liberal Answer to the Conservative Challenge*. Santa Barbara, CA: Praeger, 1965.

McElvaine, Robert G., ed. *Down and Out in the Great Depression: Letters from the Forgotten Man*. Chapel Hill: University of North Carolina Press, 1983.

Mink, Gwendolyn. *The Wages of Motherhood: Inequality in the Welfare State, 1917–1942*. Ithaca, NY: Cornell University Press, 1995.

Moynihan, Daniel Patrick. *The Negro Family: The Case for National Action*. Washington, D.C.: Office of Policy Planning and Research, U.S. Department of Labor, 1965. http://www.blackpast.org/?q=primary/moynihan-report-1965.

————. *The Politics of a Guaranteed Income: The Nixon Administration and the Family Assistance Plan*. New York: Random House, 1973.

National Opinion Research Corporation [NORC]. Roper Center for Public Opinion Research, University of Connecticut, Storrs, 1942. http://www.ropercenter.uconn.edu/data_access/ipoll/ipoll.html.

Newman, Katherine S. *Falling from Grace: Downward Mobility in an Age of Affluence*. Berkeley and Los Angeles: University of California Press, 1999.

————. *Declining Fortunes: The Withering of the American Dream*. New York: Basic Books, 1993.

Nixon, Richard M. *Public Papers of the Presidents of the United States: Richard M Nixon, 1969–1974*, vols. 1–6. Washington, DC: Government Printing Office.

Noble, Charles. *Welfare As We Knew It: A Political History of the American Welfare State*. New York: Oxford University Press, 1997.

Orleck, Annelise. *Storming Caesar's Palace: How Black Mothers Fought Their Own War on Poverty*. Boston: Beacon Press, 2005.

Page, I., and Robert Y. Shapiro. *The Rational Public: Fifty Years of Americans' Policy Preferences.* Chicago: University of Chicago Press, 1992.

Patterson, James. *America's Struggle against Poverty in the Twentieth Century.* Cambridge, MA: Harvard University Press, 2000.

Piketty, Thomas, and Emanuel Saez. "Income Inequality in the United States, 1913–1998." *Quarterly Journal of Economics* 118, no. 1 (2003): 1–39.

Pimpare, Stephen. *The New Victorians: Poverty, Politics, and Propaganda in Two Gilded Ages.* New York: New Press, 2004.

Piven, Frances Fox, and Richard Cloward. *Regulating the Poor: The Functions of Public Welfare.* New York: Vintage, 1971.

———. *The New Class War: Reagan's Attack on the Welfare State and Its Consequences.* New York: Pantheon, 1982.

Purdham, Todd. "Electoral Affirmation of Shared Values Provides Bush a Majority." *New York Times*, November 4, 2004.

Quadagno, Jill. *The Color of Welfare: How Racism Undermined the War on Poverty.* New York: Oxford University Press, 1996.

Rainwater, Lee, and William Yancey. *The Moynihan Report and the Politics of Controversy.* Cambridge, MA: MIT Press, 1967.

Rieder, Jonathan. *Canarsie: The Jews and Italians of Brooklyn against Liberalism.* Cambridge, MA: Harvard University Press, 1985.

Russell, Judith. *Economics, Bureaucracy and Race: How Keynesians Misguided the War on Poverty.* New York: Columbia University Press, 2003.

Scheve, Kenneth F, and Matthew J. Slaughter. "A New Deal for Globalization." *Foreign Affairs* July/August 2007.

Schlesinger, Arthur M., Jr. *The Crisis of the Old Order: 1919–1933, The Age of Roosevelt.* New York: Mariner Books, 2003.

Sen, Amartya. *Development as Freedom.* New York: Knopf, 1999.

Sennett, Richard and Jonathan Cobb. *The Hidden Injuries of Class.* New York: Vintage Books, 1972.

Sexton, Brendan. "Workers and Liberals: Closing the Gap." In *The White Majority: Between Poverty and Affluence*, ed. L. K. Howe. New York: Random House, 1970.

Shulman, Bruce. *From Cotton Belt to Sun Belt: Federal Policy, Economic Development, and the Transformation of the South 1938–1980.* Durham, NC: Duke University Press, 1994.

Skocpol, Theda. "Targeting Within Universalism: Politically Viable Policies to Combat Poverty in the United States." In *The Urban Underclass*, ed. C. Jencks and P. Peterson. Washington, DC: Brookings Institution Press, 1991.

————. *Protecting Soldiers and Mothers: The Political Origins of Social Policy in the United States.* Cambridge: Belknap Press of Harvard University Press, 1992.

Smith, Jason Scott. *Building New Deal Liberalism: The Political Economy of Public Works, 1933–1956.* New York: Cambridge University Press, 2005.

Steensland, Brian. *The Failed Welfare Revolution: America's Struggle over Guaranteed Income Policy.* Princeton, NJ: Princeton University Press, 2007.

Stimson, James A. *Public Opinion in America: Moods, Cycles, and Swings.* Boulder, CO: Westview Press, 1999.

Summers, Lawrence. "Unfinished Business at Fannie Mae and Freddie Mac." *Washington Post*, July 27, 2008.

Sunstein, Cass R. *The Second Bill of Rights: FDR's Unfinished Revolution and Why We Need It More Than Ever.* New York: Basic Books, 2004.

Tomasky, Michael. "Party in Search of a Notion." *American Prospect*, May 2006. www.prospect.org/web/printfriendly-view.ww?id=11424.

Teles, Steven. *Whose Welfare? AFDC and Elite Politics.* Lawrence: University Press of Kansas, 1996.

Uchitelle, Louis. "The Richest of the Rich, Proud in a New Gilded Age." *New York Times*, July 15, 2007.

Vobejda, Barbara, and Judith Havemann. "2 HHS Officials Quit Over Welfare Changes." *Washington Post*, September 12, 1996.

Watkins, T. H. *The Hungry Years: A Narrative History of the Great Depression in America.* New York: Henry Holt, 1999.

Weaver, R. Kent. *Ending Welfare As We Know It.* Washington, DC: Brookings Institution Press, 2000.

Will, Jeffry. *The Deserving Poor.* New York: Garland Publishing, 1993.

Williamson, John B., and Diane M. Watts-Roy. "Framing the Generational Equity Debate." In Williamson et al., *The Generational Equity Debate*, 3–39.

Williamson, John B., Diane M. Watts-Roy, and Eric R. Kingson, eds. *The Generational Equity Debate.* New York: Columbia University Press, 1999.

Zaller, John. *The Nature and Origins of Mass Opinion.* Cambridge: Cambridge University Press, 1992.

————. "Coming to Grips with V. O. Key's Concept of Latent Public Opinion." Paper delivered at Symposium in Honor of Phillip Converse, Boston, September 2, 1998, 13.

Zarefsky, David. *President Johnson's War on Poverty: Rhetoric and History.* Tuscaloosa: University of Alabama Press, 2005.

Zelizer, Viviana A. *The Social Meaning of Money: Pin Money, Paychecks, Poor Relief, and Other Currencies.* Princeton, NJ: Princeton University Press, 1997.

Index

The letters *t*, *f*, or *n* following a page number indicate a table, figure, or note on that page. The number following the *n* indicates the number of the note cited.